# WHAT YOU WON'T FIND IN HEAVEN

# WHAT YOU WON'T FIND
# IN HEAVEN

*A Surprising Source of Hope*

Stephen K. Moroney

WEAVER BOOK
COMPANY
WOOSTER, OHIO

First edition published by
Weaver Book Company
1190 Summerset Dr.
Wooster, OH 44691
Visit us at weaverbookcompany.com

Cover: J. R. Caines
Interior design and typesetting: { In a Word }
Editing: Line for Line Publishing Services

Print: 978-1-941337-48-6
EPUB: 978-1-941337-49-3

### Library of Congress Cataloging-in-Publication Data

Moroney, Stephen K., 1962-
    What you won't find in heaven: a surprising source of hope / Stephen K. Moroney.
—First edition.
        pages cm
    ISBN 978-1-941337-48-6
1. Heaven—Christianity. 2. Future life—Christianity. I. Title.
    BT846.3.M66 2016
    236'.24—dc23

                        2015036834

Printed in the United States of America
15 16 17 18 19 / 5 4 3 2 1

# Contents

# Acknowledgments

THIS BOOK, LIKE MOST, has been a collaborative effort. Many people read parts of the manuscript and offered constructive suggestions as I was working on it. Several members of my church also agreed to be interviewed and to have their thoughts included in the book. Special thanks to Abbey Allerding, Karelynne Ayayo, Michael Ayayo, David Beer, Kris Crosier, Ann Gardner, Joel Harris, Joy Harris, Stan Hinshaw, Bryan Hollon, Jonathan Holmes, Michael Howell-Moroney, Jillian Humphrey, Greg Jurica, Tim Keene, Jack Kragt, Roger Kunes, Margaret Moroney, Sue Moroney, Marsha Raymond, Dan Ring, Bob Robinson, Adam Romans, Sherry Shindle, Denny Thornton, Scott Waalkes, Tim Walker, and Helen Williams. Extra special thanks to Jim Weaver, who served as both the final editor and the publisher.

I want to thank the administration and trustees of Malone University for granting me a sabbatical leave in support of this book. My wife Sue's patient support, constant encouragement, and wise suggestions were indispensable at every step along the way. Above all, I thank the one who descended from heaven so that his followers might live with him forever: Jesus Christ, who reigns from heaven with the Father and the Holy Spirit, one God now and forever more.

# Introduction

WE ALL REALIZE THAT THE WORLD IS BROKEN and we long, deep down, for it to be fixed. Things are not the way they are supposed to be, but in the afterlife we hope that everything will be made right. I have ideas about what heaven will be like and so do you. Some of our ideas are pretty wild. Over the years people have told me that heaven will include infinite supplies of chocolate with no worries about fat, or heaven will feature unlimited golf with perfect swings every time.

Back in 1950, the famed evangelist Billy Graham reportedly said that in heaven "we are going to sit around the fireplace and have parties and the angels will wait on us," and "we'll drive down the golden streets in a yellow Cadillac convertible."[1] More recently, when *People* magazine asked actress Sandra Bullock what her idea of heaven was, she reportedly said, "no drama—and a pint of Häagen-Dazs," while actor Denzell Washington replied, "no kids, no noise."[2]

On a more serious note, Christian author Randy Alcorn asserted that in heaven (understood as the new heavens and new earth) we will have sex organs but no intercourse, private possessions but no greed, disagreements but no pride, business/commerce but no cheating, coffee but no caffeine addiction, movies but no approval

1  Lisa Miller, *Heaven: Our Enduring Fascination with the Afterlife* (New York: Harper Perennial, 2010), xviii.

2  *People,* vol. 61, no. 24, June 21, 2004, 142.

of sin, athletics but no sore losers, and possible minor injuries from extreme sports but always followed by full healing. After working hard in heaven to invent technology that improves our transportation, after exploring outer space and perhaps engaging in some time travel, and after breaking a good sweat while testing the limits of our resurrection bodies, according to Alcorn, we will continue to need sleep in heaven.[3]

These ideas, whether they're found in pop culture or in the more careful formulations of Christian authors, fall into the category of what is often called *theological speculation,* drifting from widely established Christian belief into the realm of opinion. But theological conjecture cannot serve as a reliable guide to heaven, nor can the recent spate of books that claim to report what heaven is like from firsthand visits there by those who returned to earth to tell about it (see appendix 1).

In figuring out what to believe about heaven, Christians naturally look to Scripture. But even here we face challenges. Many of the references to heaven are found in prophetic and apocalyptic sections of the Bible, which are notoriously difficult to interpret. What is to be taken literally and what is to be taken symbolically? For instance, are we meant to believe that heaven is a golden city measuring 1,380 miles in length, width, and height, surrounded by a pearly-gated wall? Is there an actual street of gold in heaven (Rev. 21)? Bible experts disagree about these and dozens of other interpretive questions. These debates will continue until we're on the other side.[4]

This book is different because it focuses on what is not in heaven.

---

3   Randy Alcorn, *Heaven* (Wheaton, IL: Tyndale, 2004), 297–98, 318, 338–39, 348–49, 356–57, 406–7, 410–13, 428–34. Though I have concerns about some of his speculative claims, I admire the ways Randy Alcorn has turned people's attention toward heaven, maybe more than anyone else in the past few generations.

4   In this book I try to follow the wise rule set down by past theologians to stick to what is "expressly set down in Scripture, or by good and necessary consequence may be deduced from Scripture" (*The Westminster Confession of Faith,* Chapter I, section VI). Readers will have to judge for themselves whether I successfully follow this rule.

Rather than speculating about what heaven will be like, entering academic debates, or relying on the stories of those who have supposedly been there, this book shows that we can be helped immensely by simply considering what we won't find in heaven. As we study the subject, we will be surprised at just how much Scripture has to say by way of negation. In heaven there will be no more death, mourning, crying, or pain (Rev. 21:4). There won't be any people in heaven who are cowardly, faithless, detestable, murderers, sexually immoral, sorcerers, idolaters, or liars (Rev. 21:8 and 22:15). Nothing unclean or impure will ever enter heaven, nor will anyone who does what is detestable or false (Rev. 21:27). No longer will there be anything accursed in heaven (Rev. 22:3). Radical!

This book is about how all of us live under the curse of sin now and how different, how blissfully different, things will be in heaven. A big part of that bliss is due to what is *not* in heaven. Chapter one helps us see how even a good day now, let alone a bad day, is a far cry from heaven. It also shows how heaven is the happy ending (and the new beginning!) of God's story for his world and for his people. Chapter two addresses our health issues, whether they have to do with illness, weight, or whatever troubles us physically. There will be no more of those struggles with perfect resurrection bodies in heaven!

Chapter three is about emotional issues: anxiety, depression, work problems, and family tensions. We all have headaches and heartaches now, but no one will in heaven. Chapter four explores security issues and how we long to be safe — using prisons, pepper spray, and passwords for protection. In heaven there won't be any more school shootings, stealing, or suffering for the faith, because there God's people will live securely under his reign. Chapter five addresses social issues or struggles in the economic, political, and environmental arenas. This world's problems, whether they involve terrorism, tear gas, or tsunamis, seem to be never-ending. But all the problems of the world will come to an end in heaven, which gives us life-changing hope now!

Chapter six shifts gears by taking a positive look at how heaven will be heavenly because of who *is* there—namely, God's angels, God's people, and God himself. A heavenly perspective can make a huge difference for us every day, inspiring us to live in light of eternity. The first appendix gives a fair hearing to recent bestsellers on people's supposed visits to heaven, but it also shows why these books cannot serve as reliable guides to what heaven is like. The second appendix concludes the book by answering a dozen common questions about heaven. Along the way, within each chapter, I've also included interviews in which people share some of their hard experiences in this life and what they look forward to in heaven. Heaven can touch our lives profoundly right now.

# 1

## *Earthly Life Now and Heavenly Life Later*

MY BROTHER MIKE SAYS THAT the three greatest things about my job are June, July, and August. I am a college professor, and while the school year is a busy blur of teaching, student issues, and meeting deadlines, things really slow down in the summer. But even when I'm away from the usual pressures of work in the summertime, I still live every day in a sin-stained world, under the curse. The differences between earthly life now and heavenly life later are startling. Even on a seemingly idyllic summer day, there are a lot of problems that I will no longer face in heaven.

### *A Day in My Life: Not Heaven on Earth*

It's a July Friday in Canton, Ohio. I had hoped to sleep another hour, but I realize that's not going to happen because my mind is already racing with things to tackle. I slip out of bed before sunrise. As I shower, shave, and dress I try to stay quiet so as not to wake my wife, Sue. With a glass of orange juice I wash down a daily vitamin, fish oil to help stave off memory loss, and glucosamine to soothe my joints—mainly the knee that required an ACL reconstruction. I am very grateful to have these pills, but I am pretty sure I will not need them in heaven when I'll enjoy the wonders of a resurrected body that's raised in glory and power (1 Cor. 15:43).

I have a bowl of cereal for breakfast, while spending some time in the Bible and prayer. In heaven, I probably will not need to pray any longer for my colleague's marriage that's on the rocks, my mom's health challenges, our children's jobs, our grandchild's future, or our friends who do not know Jesus as their Lord and Savior. While there will be plenty of praise in heaven (see Rev. 4, 5, and 7 for some indications), this sort of intercessory prayer that's so important now won't be needed in heaven, when God makes all things new (Rev. 21:5).

I slip on my glasses (no need for those with a resurrection body!) and sit down at the computer. Without even thinking of it, I go through the routine of logging on with a user name and password. Why do we need these precautionary steps? To guard against theft. No more of that in heaven. Imagine a world in which there will be no more worries about anyone stealing from us or deceiving us (1 Cor. 6:9–10; Rev. 21:27). I check on some investments passed down from my dad after he died from cancer last year. He was one of a kind, I was close to him, and I miss him a lot. It makes me yearn for heaven where there will be no more mourning or death (Rev. 21:4).

Next I scroll through a website on the latest in sports. I'm struck by the fact that so many of the headlines are about athletes' injuries, mostly baseball players with torn ligaments, some of them career-ending. I remember how I "retired" from my regular summer soft-ball league after a series of four injuries during a rough summer. There won't be any more pain in heaven (Rev. 21:4)!

Then I type in a different user name and password to access my email. The first item in my in-box is a request from a former student asking for a letter of recommendation in support of his pursuit of church ordination. He is a great guy with strong gifts and a long track record of faithful service. So I will have no trouble writing the letter to support him, but I don't think we'll need letters of recommendation in heaven. One reason we need them now is that we can't trust what people tell us about themselves. A misguided minister or priest can bring lasting harm to trusting people. Not in heaven. In fact, in heaven I'm pretty sure the whole ordination thing will be passé, since everyone there will serve as priests or ministers of God (Rev. 1:6; 5:10; 22:3).

Before leaving the room, I notice a piece of paper on the floor. It is part of a document I printed the night before on Mariology. I am doing some reading on the subject because I'll be serving on a panel discussing what Christians from different churches believe about Mary, mother of Jesus. Some see her as the Queen of Heaven, enjoying elite prominence in God's eternal kingdom. Others see her as an inspiring example of faith and obedience, but they don't expect Mary to be an object of unusual adoration in the afterlife. In heaven theological debate will come to an end, as every important question is answered. There we will see things clearly, rather than through a glass darkly. With the apostle Paul, all of God's people can look forward to the day when we won't just "know in part" but "shall know fully, even as I am fully known" (1 Cor. 13:12).[1]

I snap back to my to-do list and head out to the doctor's office for a follow-up appointment. As usual I am cutting it close, and I get agitated when the car in front of me actually stops at the yellow light rather than speeding through it. I had already decided to accelerate through the intersection, red light or not. Once my brakes are done protesting, I shake my head at my folly. I am thankful that in heaven I will be free of the sin that still dwells in me and clings so closely (Heb. 12:1). In heaven, we're told, the spirits of the righteous will be made perfect (Heb. 12:23).

## Further Reminders of a Fallen World

In the doctor's waiting room, I glance through the morning paper. Yesterday was a pretty quiet news day with nothing huge in the headlines, except for sports fans concerned with LeBron James and

---

1 All Scripture quotations are taken from the New International Version of the Bible.

the Cleveland Cavaliers. But when I come to the two facing pages of "Viewpoints," it is clear that we're far from heaven. A story on the abduction and murder of three Israeli teenagers launches the writer into a piece on young people who are killed on the streets of the U.S. every day. There will be no murders in heaven (Rev. 21:8). Another story details the intimidation and harassment endured by whistle-blowers who exposed abuses within the Veterans Administration. There'll be no more lying in heaven (Rev. 21:8).

The Nation & World page is filled with evidence that we're fallen people living in a fallen world. A boy died in Wisconsin after being trapped in his family's grain bin. A family of six was tied up and shot in their Texas home. A fire killed four adults and three kids in a Massachusetts apartment. A priest in Louisiana was accused of not reporting sex abuse. There will be none of that in heaven (Rev. 21:4, 8).

For a while Sue had been urging me to have a dark spot on my scalp checked. Finally I gave in. My family doctor told me nine chances out of ten it was benign, but it turned out to be malignant melanoma. Yikes! I was referred to a plastic surgeon who removed the cancerous skin, and my appointment today is a follow-up visit to remove the stitches in my head. The doctor tells me I am healing up nicely. I am very grateful to live in a time and place where this sort of procedure is practically routine. Yet I long for the day in heaven when there will be no more cancer at all.

On the way home from the doctor's office I wash the car and I receive a phone call from the dentist reminding me of my appointment on Monday. After my dentist appointment I will take my mom to see her doctor about deteriorating bone density. Then later in the afternoon I will have an appointment with my eye doctor for an annual check and to make sure that the melanoma on my scalp did not infiltrate or affect my eyes. It may not sound like it, but by God's grace, I enjoy very good overall health. In twenty-two years of teaching I've never had to cancel a class due to illness or other emergency. But even so, I sometimes need to see a family doctor, an eye doctor, a dentist, and an occasional specialist. I definitely look forward to the time when Jesus "will transform our lowly bodies so that they will be like his glorious body" (Phil. 3:21).

It's now late morning and after jotting down a few thoughts for this chapter on my laptop computer at home, it's time to hit the yard work. I'm doing a little modern-day fighting the thorns and thistles (Gen. 3:17–19)—with the help of an electric edger. My right elbow twinges and my left heel throbs, as usual. No more of those aches and pains in heaven (Rev. 21:4).

My neighbor Gus comes across the street to talk. He wants to know about our plans for a neighborhood party, which I promised but have not yet delivered. He also wants to let me know that around 3 A.M. last night, his wife, Constantina, saw a car slow down outside our homes. She heard a car door close and saw a flashlight beam into their home. This morning Gus called a home security company and he plans to install three cameras to monitor the sides of their house. We live in a decent neighborhood, but Constantina is scared, and Gus is taking preventive measures. They won't have to bother with that in heaven, where there won't be any thieves (1 Cor. 6:10) or anyone who does what is detestable or false (Rev. 21:27).

After lunch I hear a lawn mower chugging along the property behind us. I flag down my neighbor to ask if it's okay to trim the bushes that divide our yards. As we speak, another neighbor calls from his yard. To my shame, after nearly two years in our home this is my first time to meet Jim or Tony. I have to ask their names. Since the key mark of Jesus' followers is loving one another (John 13:35), I don't think these sorts of minimal relationships with our neighbors will exist in heaven. My sinful self-centeredness will be transformed in the afterlife, as God brings to completion the changes he has begun in me and all of his people (Phil. 1:6).

After dinner and relaxing with my wife, I reflect on the day. In many ways it was a nice summer day. No hassles at the office. I had access to advanced medical care and spent much of the day outside in the sun (but with a hat and plenty of sunscreen ever since my skin cancer). Many people might think of it almost as a "staycation"—a day to savor, lived in a privileged time and place in history. Yet, when I consider it, much of the day was still tainted by sin and its effects. It's striking how much of our lives is shaped by the fact that we're fallen people living in a fallen world. A good day on earth now still isn't heaven.

## *Don Bartlette's Life: Definitely Not Heaven on Earth*

While each of us can think of ways that our earthly lives now are a far cry from heaven, for some of us the contrast is more striking than for others. Think of women forced into sex trafficking, workers chained to their stations in sweat shops, or the elderly suffering with loneliness and disease in substandard nursing facilities.

Or consider the heartbreaking and inspirational life story of my acquaintance, Don Bartlette, also of Canton, Ohio.[2] Don was born with half a nose, no upper lip, and a huge hole in his mouth. His father was an alcoholic and his mother was unsure how to raise a baby with so many challenges. Early medical interventions were only partially successful and Don was unable to speak normally for most of his childhood. He faced widespread social rejection, and for his first nine years he considered rats in a nearby dump area to be his best friends. It won't be like that in heaven, when the former things pass away and all things are made new (Rev. 21:4–5).

As a poor, disabled Native American, Don was mercilessly bullied, both verbally and physically. His teacher labeled him as mentally retarded and isolated him in a janitor's closet. In one especially horrible incident, some cruel classmates tied Don to a tree and beat him bloody. When he returned home, Don was the target of more blows from his father's fists and belt. It got so bad that when his

---

2 Donald Bartlette, *Macaroni at Midnight* (Fayetteville, AR: University of Arkansas, Dept. of Social Work, 1992).

father was in a drunken stupor one night, Don determined to kill him. Don had gun in hand when his mother intervened at the last second to rescue her husband. Needless to say, these sorts of childhood experiences that Don and so many others have endured will not occur in heaven, where God will wipe away every tear from our eyes (Rev. 21:4).

With some help from others, Don persevered, graduating from high school and college. He even went on to earn multiple graduate degrees, including a doctorate in education. For the past forty years, the boy born with no upper lip and a huge hole in his mouth has served as a full-time speaker, inspiring tens of thousands with his story. That doesn't mean that everything came easily. Don himself struggled with alcoholism and abusive patterns as a husband and father. It took many years for Don to become healthy in his relationships and to forgive those who had wounded him so deeply. Even with all the growth and healing he's experienced, Don knows that the best of earthly life now does not compare to heavenly life later.

No matter how ordinary or how horrific our lives, we all long for something better, for heaven. C. S. Lewis put it this way: "If I find in myself a desire which no experience in this world can satisfy, the most probable explanation is that I was made for another world."[3] This book is about that "other world" and how what is *not* in heaven gives us a glimpse into the big picture of what God's kingdom is all about. An easy way to grasp that big picture is through considering the story of the Bible. It can be boiled down to four fast-paced scenes, with heaven as the climax.

## The First Three Scenes: Life as We Know It

Naturally, scene one is the beginning. In the very first sentence of the Bible, we read that in the beginning, God created the heavens

---

3   C. S. Lewis, *Mere Christianity* (New York: Macmillan, 1957), 106.

and the earth (Gen. 1:1). And six times we are told in Genesis 1 that everything God made was good. The pinnacle of God's creation, the very last thing God made, was humans. People are special because they are the only part of God's creation that is said to be made in God's image, after God's likeness. God is a good, wise ruler. So men and women, created in God's image and likeness, are made to function in a secondary, delegated way as good, wise rulers over the rest of creation (Gen. 1:26–28). In the beginning, everything God made, including humanity, was very good (Gen. 1:31). A good creation from a good God.

Genesis chapter 2 details how God formed the man, Adam, from the dust of the ground and breathed the breath of life into him (Gen. 2:7). God then placed the man in a lush garden to work it and take care of it (Gen. 2:15). So already in the first two chapters of the Bible—scene one of the story—we learn that people have a special role in caring for the creation of which they are a part. Humans enjoy God-given freedom but they also have God-given limits—a tree from which they must not eat, with a warning about the dire consequences of transgressing their limits (Gen. 2:16–17).

Scene two is when things start to fall apart. People were made to obey their Creator, but instead they disobey his command (Gen. 3:6), which has some serious fallout. Eve is the mother of all the living (Gen. 3:20), but she'll bring forth children in pain (Gen. 3:16). Adam is supposed to care for the garden (Gen. 2:15), but there will be painful toil as he works with a ground that is now cursed with thorns and thistles (Gen. 3:17–19). Adam and Eve originally enjoyed a great, open relationship (Gen. 2:18–25), but with the entrance of sin, they begin to experience shame, blame, and relational struggle (Gen. 3:7–16). What was very good becomes seriously tainted.

And it only gets worse. Before long there is cold-blooded murder within the family, brother against brother (Gen. 4:8). Vengeful violence characterizes people (Gen. 4:23–24). We are told in Genesis 6:5 "how great the wickedness of the human race had become on the earth" and how "every inclination of the thoughts of the human heart was only evil all the time." It gets so bad that God decides to wipe the slate clean with a flood and begin over with Noah's family (Gen. 6–7). But sin has brought about a fundamental change in people, so much so that even after the fresh post-flood start we are told "every inclination of the human heart is evil from childhood" (Gen. 8:21).

If this mess is going to be cleaned up, God will have to be the one to do it. In his great wisdom and mercy, God unfolds a masterful plan to use Abram (later renamed Abraham) to bless all the families of the earth (Gen. 12:1–3). The rest of the Old Testament can be read as an overlapping mixture of scene two (people sinfully disobeying God) and scene three (God carrying out his plan to bless people worldwide through Abraham's descendants, including the Messiah).

There are many twists and turns in the plot along the way. Though God's people are enslaved in Egypt, God miraculously uses Moses to deliver them and gives them commandments by which to live. God leads them into the Promised Land under Joshua. God raises up judges and kings to lead his people. God patiently endures the people's sinful worship of idols. But after centuries of repeated disobedience, God finally exiles his people from the land by the hands of the Assyrians and Babylonians, before bringing them back to their homeland under the rule of the Persians.

Israel's prophets warn them that God judges sin, and they urge the people to repent. The prophets also promise that there will be a future restoration through a coming Messiah who will save his people. The Old Testament points forward to Jesus Christ, who reveals God in ways that had been only shadowy before (John 1:18; 14:6–11). Though scene two (humans' warped life of sin) is long and dark, scene three (God's plan of salvation through Jesus the Messiah) brings light and hope that things can be restored. By his miraculous birth, profound teaching, compassionate healing, gathering disciples, seeking the lost, living sinlessly, dying for others, and rising again triumphantly, Jesus fulfills what the Old Testament had promised (Luke 24:25–27, 44–47).

## The Final Climactic Scene: Life in Heaven

The apostle Paul writes several letters that have a lot to say about heaven—the final scene in God's story. The Christians in Corinth are told that "just as we have borne the image of the earthly man, so shall we bear the image of the heavenly man" (1 Cor. 15:49). We are like Adam, the earthly human, in that we're created in God's image, but we've fallen into sin as Adam did. Jesus' followers, however, were also created to bear his image as the heavenly man. Paul says God is working everything together for his people's good, to make us like Jesus (Rom. 8:28–29).

In Paul's mind, the heavenly future of God's people is assured. As he puts it, using the certainty of the past tense, God has "blessed us in the heavenly realms with every spiritual blessing in Christ" (Eph. 1:3). Again, using the past tense, Paul says believers have been raised up and seated with Christ in the heavenly places (Eph. 2:6). And ultimately the outcome of that spiritual battle is certain, according to Paul, because at the name of Jesus every knee will bow, in heaven and on earth and under the earth (Phil. 2:10). While heaven is already a future certainty, it has not yet arrived in its fullness. So Jesus' followers await his return from heaven (1 Thess. 4:16).

The destiny of Christians is so closely tied to heaven that Paul says our fundamental citizenship is in heaven (Phil. 3:20). While it's true that Jesus' followers are temporary citizens of many different nation-states, our ultimate allegiance and identification should not be to a Chinese premier, an American president, or an Indian prime minister, but rather to Jesus Christ who will return from heaven. According to Paul, our highest master is in heaven (Col. 4:1), and we eagerly await the time when Jesus will come back from heaven to reign as king (1 Thess. 1:10).

The author of the book of Hebrews had a perspective similar to Paul's. Hebrews characterizes God's people as "foreigners and strangers on earth" or people who "are looking for a country of their own" (11:13–14). More specifically, "they were longing for a better country—a heavenly one" (Heb. 11:16a). Therefore, because they are seeking a heavenly country, "God is not ashamed to be called their God, for he has prepared a city for them" (Heb. 11:16b). Later the author describes this as "the city of the living God, the heavenly Jerusalem . . . the church of the firstborn, whose names are written in heaven" (Heb. 12:22–23). The author adds at the end that "here we do not have an enduring city, but we are looking for the city that is to come" (Heb. 13:14). God's people are reminded from Scripture that no matter where we live now, our true home is the heavenly city that God has prepared for his people.

Heaven is the climactic fourth and final scene in God's story. It can be pictured as God restoring what we have messed up—an extreme makeover. Paul says that due to sin "the whole creation has been groaning as in the pains of childbirth right up to the present" (Rom. 8:22), but with the hope that someday it will be freed from the curse of sin and all its negative effects. In the last chapter of the Bible, John says that in the new heavens and the new earth "no longer will there be any curse" (Rev. 22:3). The curse will be reversed! The new heavens and the new earth are the way things are supposed to be—the final scene that brings resolution to the divine drama.

Heaven is the joyous ending (and, in another sense, the breathtaking beginning) to the story for God's people. We will experience the new heavens and the new earth as the perfect eternal home God has prepared for us (2 Pet. 3:13; Rev. 21:1). In the pages ahead we'll see hundreds and hundreds of ways that heaven will be heavenly because of what is *not* there. There is so much wrong with the world as we experience it now, but in heaven every wrong will be made right!

*For Individual Reflection or Group Discussion*

1. As you begin this study on heaven, what is something you are excited or curious about?

2. Think back to a day in the past week, and jot down some of the things you experience in your earthly life now that God's people will not have to deal with in heavenly life later.

3. Reflect on or describe the person you know who is most like Don Bartlette, a personal acquaintance of yours whose life has been really hard and is definitely not heaven on earth.

4. What aspect of heaven (scene four in God's story) is especially appealing or attractive to you?

*Interview with Adam Romans*

**Brief Bio:** Adam has been in the ministry for fifteen years and he serves as the lead pastor at my church. I am privileged to hear him preach, work with him as an elder, and enjoy him as a friend.

*What has been the hardest thing about your experience on earth as a pastor?*

The hardest thing is seeing important family relationships and friendships fall apart. Sadly, I have watched long marriages end for both very simple and extremely complex reasons. Siblings sometimes will no longer engage in each other's life. I find it especially sad when a child and parent relationship is unreconciled or when close friends will no longer speak to each other. We were not meant to live without these important relationships and it is difficult to watch them crumble when harmful words or deeds unnecessarily end them.

*From your perspective as a pastor, what do you most look forward to in heaven?*

As a pastor, the thing I look forward to the most in heaven is the absence of sin. Sin affects everything and is the root cause of all evil, disease, and everything that is wrong in our world. I love the text in Revelation 21, which describes a new heaven and a new earth free from death, mourning, pain, and so on. Our world is broken and knowing Jesus will one day make it new and right brings great hope. I look forward to heaven because, among other things, our relationships with God and each other will be free from messes, cancer will be gone, wars will cease, and sin will be no more.

*Share a time when, as a pastor, you had at least a "glimpse of heaven on earth."*

I am not sure if I have ever really experienced a taste of heaven on earth. The most "heavenly experiences" that I recall are moments of powerful worship with God's people, standing amazed at God's creation on top of a mountain, and enjoying rich communion with God privately.

## Interview with Jillian Humphrey

**Brief Bio:** Jillian has been at home mostly full-time with her two children (and those of friends) for the past five years. She regularly shares wise insights with our Bible study leaders at church.

*What has been the hardest thing about your experience on earth as a mom with two little kids?*

Prior to becoming a mom, I envisioned that my children would require my strengths: my peacefulness, my compassion, my tenderness, and other maternal virtues. But both of my children have required my weaknesses much more than my strengths. I've had to be patient with interruptions, restore order to loud, high-energy chaos, adapt to constant and unexpected change, and function well without sleep, silence, or solitude. Over the past five years, I have continually functioned outside my sphere of competency and comfort, and with so much at stake. This has felt terrifying, overwhelming, and impossible in turns.

*From your perspective as a mother and wife, what do you most look forward to in heaven?*

Many days my work as a stay-at-home mom feels futile, invisible, and lonely. I am thwarted at every turn. I bring order only to have it brought into disorder. I discipline for the same unkindness over and over. I want to add beauty but feel conflicted about how consumerism shapes my understanding of it. All of this laboring makes me long, acutely and chronically, for a home where my work is rest and peace, not vanity or toil. I cannot wait to hear "welcome home, much-loved child." I long for this even more than "well done, good and faithful servant." I find comfort in John 14 and 17, when Jesus states that his deep desire is to have us at home with him. He prepares a place for us, and his desire is not simply to take us to a place, but to take us to himself. Home.

*Share a time when, as a stay-at-home mom, you had at least a "glimpse of heaven on earth."*

I get at least a few glimpses of heaven on earth daily. One of my favorite images is a memory of my daughter, Anna, chasing robins in our back yard. It was a perfect June day — warm, sunny with puffy white clouds. She ran barefoot in and out of the shade of a giant oak and called, "Come here, birdie! Come here, birdie!" with the kind of uninhibited joy and playful delight that I imagine God possesses all the time and to an infinite degree.

# 2 Health Issues: No More Hospitals, Heart Disease, or Hospice

## The Mind-Boggling Human Body

The human body is amazing. We each start out as a single cell that divides into two, four, eight, sixteen, and eventually trillions of cells. As these cells differentiate, they make us who we are. Once we're grown, roughly fifty billion cells die in our bodies every day, but they are replaced by approximately fifty billion new cells that our bodies produce each day. Astonishing!

As we learn in grade school, we have five primary senses. After the first three months of life our eyes grow very little in size, but they are capable of distinguishing more than a million different color subtleties, and they give us massive amounts of information. By contrast, our noses never stop growing and they can detect at least ten thousand different scents. It goes way beyond distinguishing pungent blue cheese from fresh-cut grass or cigar smoke from woody pine. Our ears also never stop growing and they capture a myriad of sound waves that the brain interprets.

Everybody's tongue has a unique print, just like their fingers. Imagine using that for our background checks! The tongue and other parts of the mouth and throat are covered with approximately ten thousand taste buds that enable us to enjoy an incredible array of flavor sensations. A tiny portion of our fingertip skin contains thousands of touch receptors and nerve endings that flood our brains with information about pain, pressure, temperature, and texture.

Our nervous systems send impulses at a speed of over one hundred miles per hour to and from our brains. Each of our kidneys contains an estimated one million individual filters called nephrons. Although the average body contains between one and one and a half gallons of blood, if you measure the total volume pumped by the heart, it adds up to nearly two thousand gallons each day. And that's nothing compared to the roughly sixty thousand miles of vessels through which our blood flows—enough in every single person to circle the earth a couple of times.

Clearly we are fearfully and wonderfully made (Ps. 139:14). But just as clearly, a lot can go wrong with our bodies. Helen Keller is a dramatic case. Though she was able to hear and see for the first nineteen months of her life, an illness she suffered before her second birthday took away her hearing and sight. With the help of her patient and intuitive teacher Anne Sullivan, Helen eventually learned to communicate in powerful ways. But she always remained deaf and blind.

Most of us do not face hurdles in any way comparable to those that Helen Keller overcame. In a recent visit to the dentist I was required to complete a history that listed seventy-seven possible health problems. Thankfully I was able to check "no" to seventy-five of them and "yes" to just two. But we all realize that, no matter how healthy we may be, our bodies are far from perfect and we are all undergoing a process of physical decay that will inevitably lead to death. As the apostle Paul put it, "outwardly we are wasting away" (2 Cor. 4:16).

## A Friendly Visit to the Hospital

As I work on this chapter I decide to make a friendly (non-patient) visit to the emergency room of Mercy Medical Center, a local hospital in Canton, Ohio. I have situated myself in an inconspicuous spot, as far as I can get from the televisions blaring in the corners of the waiting room. Five of the people seeking treatment are in wheelchairs, two use crutches, and another leans on a cane. I don't think we'll need those sorts of devices in heaven, where we are told that our bodies, which are "sown in weakness," will be "raised in power" (1 Cor. 15:43).

A baby with a hospital band around his chubby little wrist is the first patient summoned by the nurse. Seeing the baby disappear behind the foreboding double doors takes me back to the panic that Sue and I felt as our infant daughter, Joy, strained to get oxygen into her lungs, requiring us to rush her in for a life-sustaining breathing treatment. Now Joy is grown up, married, and caring for a daughter of her own. Parents worry all the time about whether their kids will simply survive to see adulthood. It's nice to know there will be no worries about sick babies in heaven.

As I write, it's early in the evening on a Tuesday in July, the end of a beautiful sunny day. Inside the ER waiting room, things are not as beautiful. Everyone is either hurting in some way or accompanying someone who is hurting. Otherwise they wouldn't be here. A man two chairs in front of me vomits into a pan. After he moves to the space between the sliding entry doors, a security guard asks him to not lie down there. An older woman — probably his mother — curses the security officer for his lack of sympathy. There will be no more of these situations in heaven.

I am thankful for places like Mercy Medical Center and the people who serve in them. The staff members are cordial and efficient at getting patients through the system. By God's grace, modern medicine has come a long way. I have read that today, a person can survive even after having their spleen, stomach, a kidney, and most of their intestines and liver removed. I'm thankful to live in such times, but medical advances will never overcome the curse of sin and the resulting bodily decay, disease, and death which sin brought into the world (Gen. 3; Rom. 5).

I am proud that my maternal great-grandfather was a pastor but I am saddened that he died of heart failure. Heart disease remains the leading cause of death among both men and women. Every 35–45 seconds, less than the time it takes to read this page, someone in the U.S. has a heart attack.

Then there's cancer. My recent melanoma was one of more than 1.5 million new cancer cases diagnosed in the U.S. that year. Annually more than a half million Americans die from cancer, as my father did. There's breast cancer, lung cancer, prostate cancer, colorectal cancer, skin cancer, bladder cancer, kidney cancer, pancreatic cancer, lymphoma, leukemia, and many other ugly types of cancer. We all know people who've battled these diseases and some who have died from them. Part of what will make heaven heavenly is that there will be no more heart failure or cancer there. The perishable earthly bodies of God's people will be raised imperishable (1 Cor. 15:42).

Heart disease and cancer are just two of the conditions treated at Mercy Medical Center. Anemia, arthritis, asthma, blood diseases, breathing problems, convulsions, diabetes, emphysema, epilepsy, hepatitis, hypoglycemia, kidney problems, liver disease, lung disease, osteoporosis, rheumatism and rheumatic fever, scarlet fever, shingles, sickle cell disease, stomach or intestinal diseases, thyroid disease, tuberculosis, tumors, and ulcers are just a small sampling of the sorts of physical afflictions that bring people to this hospital for care.

The hospital offers concussion management, a Coumadin clinic, dialysis services, an emergency chest pain center, grief and support services, hospice care, an intensive care unit, an internal medicine clinic, orthopedic services, ostomy care, pain management, palliative care, pediatric therapy, pulmonary rehabilitation, radiology services, robotic surgery, a sleep center, speech and language therapy, a spine care program, a stroke center, a vascular center, a vestibular rehabilitation program, and a wound care center. No need for these services in heaven, where God's people are promised that our natural bodies will be raised as glorified spiritual bodies (1 Cor. 15:44).

Mercy Medical is only one of approximately five thousand hospitals in the U.S. Globally there are a few hundred thousand hospitals, though the World Health Organization counts less than twenty thousand as having registered a commitment to hand hygiene. Some developing countries do not have what most of us would consider a single sanitary hospital in their entire nation. I'm thankful for many good hospitals here in the U.S., but I'm even happier that there won't be any hospitals in heaven. As I power down my laptop and walk to my car in the parking deck of Mercy Medical Center, my heart longs for the day when every single person in heaven will be healthy for ever and ever, with no worries about pain or death (Rev. 21:4).

## Health-care and Heaven

No matter what you think about our health-care system, there's no denying that we devote a staggering amount of energy and resources to fighting the effects of the fall on our bodies. Health-care represents more than a sixth of the gross domestic product in the U.S., at an annual average of $9,000 per person, by far the highest per capita spending on medical expenses in the world. Medical bills are now a leading cause of personal bankruptcy. In heaven we won't have any concerns about pre-existing conditions. We won't have to worry about who is in network, how big our deductibles are, or affording co-pays. There is no HIPAA in heaven!

The CDC reports that there are more than fifty million inpatient surgery procedures performed in the U.S. every year. Many of these are routine, minor surgeries. Then again, as the joke goes, minor surgery is what happens to someone else. If it's me or my loved one, it's major. In heaven there will be no more operations. No more worries about something going wrong with the anesthesia. No more staples or stitches to hold us together while we heal. No more recovery or rehabilitation regimens. In heaven, Jesus' followers are promised that our Savior will powerfully "transform our lowly bodies so that they will be like his glorious body" (Phil. 3:21).

Then there are the pills. Abilify for depression, bipolar, and mood disorders. Nexium to counteract acid reflux. Humira and Enbrel to combat arthritis and other joint problems. Crestor to target cholesterol and heart problems. Advair to work against asthma attacks and breathing problems. Remicade to fight Crohn's disease, colitis, and arthritis. Cymbalta to help with depression, anxiety, and pain disorders. Each one of these drugs, by themselves, had sales in the range of $4–6 billion in the U.S. last year. And they're just the tip of the iceberg. In heaven there will be no more prescription pads, pharmacies, or pills. No more medicine, period, unless you count the leaves from the tree of life that are for the healing of the nations, which likely refers to leaves that "give health to all" rather than "heal bodily disease" (Ezek. 47:12; Rev. 22:2).

Besides the medical issues associated with our bodies, there are all the crazy things we're willing to try to enhance our physical appearance in this life. When channel surfing, I have breezed past infomercials for body shapers to redirect free-roaming fat, suction devices for plumper lips, the thigh master ($100 million in sales), wrinkle creams, and even spray-on hair to cover bald spots. "But wait! There's more!" I'd be shocked if our resurrection bodies needed any of these fad-conscious "improvements." My best guess is that in heaven we won't have any interest in them, where our bodies that are "sown in dishonor" will be "raised in glory" (1 Cor. 15:43).

Speaking of fads, I would also guess that there will be no fad diets in heaven. Snacking on cotton balls to curb your hunger or purposely ingesting tapeworms sounds sketchy, if not dangerous. Consuming five hundred calories per day while being injected with someone else's hormones doesn't have the ring of common sense, but it shows that people will try just about anything to lose weight. Any given week, approximately one-fifth of Americans report being on diets, many of which are scientifically sound and needed. Still, I think there's a very good chance that number will drop to zero in heaven, where God's people will enjoy healthy resurrection bodies.

While fad infomercials and outlandish diet plans may be comical, American culture's obsession with food, weight loss, and body image is no laughing matter. When Sue and I were earning our master's degrees in clinical psychology, we interned at a hospital eating disorders unit, where we worked with people battling anorexia, bulimia, compulsive overeating, and other related problems. It's heartbreaking to see an average-height woman who weighs under one hundred pounds look in a mirror with the conviction that she is fat. Or to hear a teenager tell about binge eating an entire cake in ten minutes followed by self-induced vomiting. No more of that in heaven either.

Body image is a huge concern for people in this life. When I saw the plastic surgeon to have my skin cancer removed, I read the list of services provided there, which includes a menu of procedures to tighten, tuck, enlarge, lift, smooth, and shrink practically every conceivable human part. What a relief to know that in heaven our spiritual bodies will be whole and healthy (1 Cor. 15). Bette Midler is not a trained theologian but she's on to something when she says, "Heaven would be a place where people would stop talking about their weight and what they look like."[1]

## Dentists, Childbirth, and Pain

As a kid I wore braces for three years, complete with the head gear at night. When I hit twenty-one, it was time to have my wisdom teeth extracted. Mine were done the old-fashioned way, with local anesthesia and pliers. It wasn't too bad until my lower left tooth cracked in half, making my already woozy head spin faster. The dentist spent what seemed like hours trying to get a grip on the partial tooth still embedded in my gums. By the time he was done, I wished I had opted for oral surgery. Foolishly, I had braved the whole experience alone and drove myself home, though still in an altered state from the drugs and the pain.

---

1  *People,* vol. 61, no. 24, June 21, 2004, 142.

Recently the dentist recommended that I have three teeth re-capped. The first time was not pleasant, and I don't relish the thought of round two. Of course, it's pretty small potatoes in the big scheme of things, but I'm glad there will be no more dental pain in heaven. No more cavities, fillings, root canals, crowns, extractions, bridges, or implants. Probably not even teeth whitening! And what of the dentists themselves? Whether or not you believe the claims about high suicide rates among dentists, it's a sure thing they will no longer have to cause others pain in heaven, even if the temporary pain they cause on earth is a wise tradeoff for all the good they do. Dental problems and pain are part of the former things that pass away in heaven (Rev. 21:4).

The subject of enduring temporary pain for a greater good brings childbirth to mind. I have vivid memories of the days our two daughters were born. Mine are mostly memories of amazement and thankfulness to God. Sue's memories, though, are more mixed. Yes, there is the immense joy of giving birth and the incredible wonder of holding that newborn! But there are also the unforgettable labor pains, coming on the heels of all the discomforts of pregnancy. Genesis 3:16 famously records God's proclamation to the woman that as a consequence of her sin "I will make your pains in childbearing very severe; with painful labor you will give birth to children."

The very act of bringing forth new life is usually mixed with pain here on earth, the miracle of epidurals notwithstanding. Our youngest daughter recently went through thirty-four hours of labor before delivering our first grandchild. Her husband was a fantastic coach, but it was long and arduous. As I write this, our oldest daughter is pregnant, with the labor ahead of her. In heaven there will be no more pain (Rev. 21:4). Presumably, that also includes the pain and trouble most women endure during their monthly cycles. No more cramps in heaven!

Temporary pain is one thing. Pain that never leaves is quite another. Over the past year I've struggled with constant low-level TMJ pain in my right jaw, and my experience is nothing compared with what others endure. Though estimates vary, several studies indicate that as many as three out of ten Americans live with chronic pain in their lower backs, necks, heads (including migraines), and elsewhere. Pain management teams can sometimes help, but many people just have to accept that they will be in pain for the rest of their earthly lives.

As though decades of quadriplegia weren't enough, Joni Eareckson Tada has spent the past several years in a war with nonstop pain, "sometimes slow and grinding, sometimes white-hot and seemingly unbearable."[2] Though she is paralyzed and has no feeling in her limbs, somehow Joni is able to experience agonizing pain in her lower back and hip. She worries about wearing out her friends and loving husband who care for her amidst what sometimes feels like a losing battle. Joni, and many others, cherish God's iron-clad promise that there will be no more pain of any kind in heaven (Rev. 21:4), but instead a resounding victory in Christ (1 Cor. 15:57).[3]

### Good Things Gone Bad

Most of us are also affected, directly or indirectly, by the pain surrounding physical addictions to nicotine, various drugs, and alcohol. Wine has its place in God's good creation, as something God has provided for us to enjoy. After all, Jesus turned water into high-quality wine (John 2:7–11) and Paul told Timothy to take a little wine for his stomach ailment (1 Tim. 5:23). Jesus even indicates that he will drink the fruit of the vine with his followers in the coming kingdom of God (Mark 14:25). But many of us, including me as a teenager, have taken a good thing and misused it, putting ourselves

---

2  Joni Eareckson Tada, *A Place of Healing: Wrestling with the Mysteries of Suffering, Pain, and God's Sovereignty* (Colorado Springs, CO: David C. Cook, 2010), 20.

3  Among many others, note the story of a woman "who struggled for years with debilitating chronic pain, and for whom this verse [Rev. 21:4] with its promise [no more pain] was her daily lifeline to sanity" in Bruce Milne, *The Message of Heaven and Hell: Grace and Destiny* (Downers Grove, IL: InterVarsity Press, 2002), 314.

and others in danger through drunk driving and other hurtful activities under the influence. We can affirm with Paul that "everything God created is good" (1 Tim. 4:4), and we can look forward to heaven, where we will no longer use good things in bad ways. Another good thing that is all too often misused is our sexuality. Originally in the Garden of Eden, we are told "Adam and his wife were both naked, and they felt no shame" (Gen. 2:25). Sexual intimacy within a lifelong covenant commitment is one of God's many gifts to people. But once sin enters the picture, we misuse this gift in ways God never intended. Just this week our local paper ran a story on a man in our neighborhood who pleaded guilty to three decades of illegally taking pictures of nude minors (boys, aged 6–16), as well as criminal child enticement for trying to get children to go with him for the purpose of sexual gratification. Despite several families' pleas for a longer prison term, he was sentenced to just five years. There will be no such worries about sexual immorality in heaven (Rev. 21:8; 22:15). Again we're reminded that a big reason heaven will be heavenly is because of what is *not* there.

## The Defeat of Death

In closing this chapter about body issues, it's fitting to include a few words about bodily death. Country musician Kenny Chesney speaks for many when he sings, "Everybody wanna go to heaven but nobody wanna go now." Two-thirds of Americans believe that heaven is a real place, not just a concept,[4] but most of us want to stay as far away from death as possible.

Comedian Woody Allen quipped, "I'm not afraid of death; I just don't want to be there when it happens." We know that death is inevitable, but we try to push it out of our minds. In a sequel to his

4 http://ligonier-static-media.s3.amazonaws.com/uploads/thestateof theology/TheStateOfTheology-FullSurveyKeyFindings.pdf. Retrieved 10/3/15.

Pulitzer prize-winning book on the subject, author Ernest Becker argued that "societies are standardized systems of *death denial*."[5] We strive collectively to avoid this sobering reality.

The Bible, however, talks about death quite often. It recognizes that death is sorrowful for the relatives and friends of the deceased. Jesus wept in response to Lazarus's death (John 11:32–36) and devout Christians mourned deeply for Stephen after his death (Acts 8:2). While we grieve our loved ones, we also have great hope for those who die in Christ (1 Thess. 4:13; 5:10). Those who trust in God need not fear death (Heb. 2:14–15), which can give us a radical perspective on life. After being stoned and left for dead, Paul simply moved on to the next town and preached the same gospel for which he had been nearly killed (Acts 14:19–22). Why? For him to live was Christ and to die was gain, something to which he looked forward (Phil 1:20–23).

The Bible teaches the bad news that human death is a result of sin (Rom. 5:12–21; 6:23). But the Bible also teaches the good news that Jesus has atoned for the sins of his people, dying the death we deserve and then rising victoriously, so that all who trust in Jesus can share in his victory over death. Paul says that "the last enemy to be destroyed is death" (1 Cor. 15:26), and God gives his people victory over death through the Lord Jesus Christ (1 Cor. 15:54–57). John brings us the same good news as Paul, that in heaven "there will be no more death" (Rev. 21:4).

In heaven we won't need any of the services of the "death care industry," a $15 billion business annually in the U.S., where there are hundreds of casket sellers, more than one thousand crematories, approximately twenty thousand funeral homes, and more than one hundred thousand cemeteries. In heaven no one will study mortuary science and there won't be any more annual conventions and expos for vendors to display the latest trends in coffins, crypts, cremation, and comforting the bereaved.

---

5    Ernest Becker, *Escape from Evil* (New York: Free Press, 1975), 153–54.

## 2. Health Issues

Sometimes death is almost a welcome relief, as it was for my maternal grandfather who was suffering after a full life at age 104. Other times it seems premature, as when sudden cancer took my otherwise healthy dad before he and my stepmom could enjoy all they had planned for their retirement years. It's especially hard when children die or babies die before they are born. The following poem by mother April Westlake provides a touching contrast between the aching death of a little one before birth and the joyous life all of God's people can anticipate in heaven later.

> I never got to hold you,
> Or kiss your little head.
> Or watch you sleeping soundly,
> All snuggled in your bed.
>
> I can't count your tiny fingers,
> Or your even smaller toes.
> I won't see your smile,
> Or your cute little button nose.
>
> You're gone too soon — we don't even know,
> If you're a girl or boy.
> Our hearts are filled with sorrow,
> When they should be full of joy.
>
> I know you are in heaven,
> Where there is no pain or tears.
> You'll never get hurt or sick,
> In heaven there are no fears.
>
> And though I'm sad you're not here right now,
> For us to hold today.
> I know we'll hold you in our arms
> When we're in heaven with you someday.[6]

6 http://www.familyfriendpoems.com/poem/losing-a-baby-isnt-easy-my
-little-angel#ixzz3Nlk99ha7. Retrieved 10/3/15.

31

## For Individual Reflection or Group Discussion

1. What do you find most amazing about how God has designed the human body to work?

2. In light of the biggest physical challenges you face every day, ponder what 1 Corinthians 15:42–44 says about our earthly bodies now and people's resurrection bodies in heaven.

3. Describe a fad approach that you have taken in an effort to improve your physical appearance, and consider how 1 Samuel 16:7 and Philippians 3:20–21 speak to our body-image issues.

4. Reflect on or tell about your most powerful experience with death and explain how God is able to provide victory in the midst of that experience (1 Cor. 15:50–58).

*Interview with Roger Kunes*

**Brief Bio:** Roger has served as a physician assistant for more than a decade and trains upcoming physician assistants at the University of Mount Union. He is a treasured elder-in-training at our church.

*What has been the hardest thing about your experience on earth as a physician assistant?*

One of the toughest things for me is being unable to correct someone's chronic illness, when I can provide only temporary relief but with no hope of cure. Even more jarring are the physical and emotional injuries that are self-inflicted or inflicted on others by sinful drunkenness or abuse. On the night shift in the ER I saw a beautiful young woman who had been punched in the face and pushed out of a moving vehicle by her intoxicated husband, causing her a severe head injury. I also remember a man who drank so much he fell backward off the barstool and broke his neck. I hate seeing these kinds of situations.

*From your perspective as a health-care provider, what do you most look forward to in heaven?*

I most look forward to the absence of pain, suffering, and death in heaven. It is not uncommon in the emergency department to have a family rush in upon the news of a family member who is dying or who has just died. There is so much agonizing and severe grief expressed in these hours. In heaven there will be no more death, dying, mourning, or crying. Thanks be to God.

*Share a time when, as a physician assistant, you had at least a "glimpse of heaven on earth."*

I've had the privilege of assisting in orthopedic surgeries, including total hip replacements. Many of these patients can't walk without significant limping and debilitating pain, but once their hip is replaced they are often up and walking the same day without any pain. I have also assisted an orthopedic spine surgeon in removing herniated disk and bone spur material off the spinal cord and spinal nerves, giving patients complete relief of their pain and weakness. They have been completely restored without pain or weakness. The patient's relief and joy of being cured has been a glimpse of the joy of heaven for me.

### Interview with Ann Gardner

**Brief Bio:** Ann is a nurse who works with post-op patients during their transition after surgery. She lived with us one summer and she is a valued member of my wife's Bible study small group.

*What has been the hardest thing about your experience on earth as a nurse?*

Quite honestly, nearly every day is hard, as I am faced with the effects of sicknesses that draw people closer and closer to death. The body can be put through an intense degree and heavy amount of suffering. One of the hardest things is people who are dying or enduring a terminal illness without adequate pain relief. As a nurse, my desire is to help and comfort. When I can't help in the way I desire, I feel powerless. It's also hard to see the hopelessness in many of my patients but not be able to address their relationship with God because my professional role does not always allow or call for me to share my faith or thoughts regarding their spiritual situation.

*From your perspective as a health-care provider, what do you most look forward to in heaven?*

What I most look forward to in heaven is being free from all illness and suffering. We will no longer gasp for air, face pain from the cancer eating away our bodies, or feel the ache when our loved ones leave us too early. We will dwell with the Great Physician who knows exactly what is going on in our bodies. No more guessing games or rounds of multiple testing without clear answers. I look forward to when our Father in heaven really will make it all better!

*Share a time when, as a nurse, you had at least a "glimpse of heaven on earth."*

I think of times that I have seen people literally be the hands and feet of Jesus. Family members have sacrificed so much of their time, energy, and effort to pour all of themselves into caring and loving my patients. They have had many sleepless nights but somehow show up where they are needed. They have rubbed sore feet and sung favorite songs. I have seen Christ through many husbands as they loved their wives through an illness. They have been such tangible examples of the way that Christ loves the church—always with her to guide her and protect her. Selfless love is rare in this world, but when I get a glimpse of it I see a beautiful reflection of the Lord.

# 3

## Emotional Issues: No More Personal Problems, Work Worries, or Family Feuds

SHORTLY AFTER MY DAD'S SIXTEENTH BIRTHDAY, his father committed suicide. It wasn't a quiet overdose in the bathroom or a car left running in the garage. It was a very public event. The Associated Press story, which ran in several newspapers, detailed how this prominent oilman and attorney plunged headfirst to his death from atop an 11-story building in Dallas. Though I never knew my paternal grandfather, clearly he was facing heavy personal issues, just as my dad faced many of his own psychological challenges over the years. At different points in our lives, nearly all of us struggle with emotional problems, and for a lot of us anxiety is at the top of the list.

### Anxiety

According to the National Institute of Mental Health, some forty million adults in the U.S., nearly one in five, suffer from an anxiety disorder. Anxiety issues are all around us. Many people have strong fears when they are in the presence of, or simply anticipating, a particular object, place, or situation. Phobias can develop suddenly, even out of the blue, when people encounter specific animals (spiders, snakes, and dogs), driving or flying, elevators or other small spaces, germs, heights, medical procedures, thunder/lightning, and other experiences. Anxiety runs pretty strong in my mom's half of the family and it hit me hard and unexpectedly in my late 30s.

Looking back at my journal entries in the fall of 1999, I can see that I was much, much too busy. I took on too many responsibilities and was rushing from pressure to pressure through nearly every day. It culminated when a photocopier broke and I ended up running to a conference presentation, arriving out of breath, literally seconds before my paper was scheduled. I began my talk still shaky and hyperventilating. I couldn't get through an entire sentence without gulping for oxygen. I grew dizzy and faint before asking for a switch of presentation order. I sat down in embarrassment after my public panic attack—the first I had ever experienced, but not the last.

Though I hoped it might be just an isolated one-time incident, anxiety struck again a few months later before I spoke to a thousand students at our university chapel. I asked the Lord for a peace that passes all understanding. I specifically prayed for God to control and calm my spirit and my body—heart, mind, and mouth. The morning of my chapel message, however, my heart raced and my head spun. I told my wife Sue about my anxiety and asked if she'd be willing to finish my message if I had a full-blown attack. In the end I made it through the talk, but I was shaky.

Anxiety continued to rear its ugly head at unwanted times, usually associated with public speaking or reading. That's not a good thing for a college professor! It got so bad I even dreaded being called on to read a Bible passage out loud in Sunday school. So I began seeing a Christian psychologist who took me through a program of anxiety de-escalation, for which I'm very grateful. I sometimes still get nervous before addressing large groups, but I'm thankful that, by God's grace and with some expert help, anxiety no longer dominates my day-to-day functioning.

Social anxiety disorder strikes fear into fifteen million Americans who dread being scrutinized or judged by others in social situations. People with this problem worry so much about making mistakes or looking bad in front of others that they may avoid or minimize interacting with people. Even something as common at eating with others, talking on the phone, or speaking in a small group can make them uneasy. It goes way beyond being shy or not wanting to be the center of attention to thinking that everyone is looking at you or being terrified that you may embarrass or humiliate yourself. I knew a lady who had it so bad that for several years she almost never came out of her house. Her husband always flew solo at social events.

Generalized anxiety disorder manifests itself in excessive worry about everyday things such as money, health, family, or work. Just to take the first item in the list, more than half of all Americans worry about not having enough money for retirement, not being able to cover medical costs, and not being able to pay off monthly bills or bigger debts. Sometimes these concerns are realistic, but in other cases we fret over things unnecessarily. Anxieties of all types cast a long shadow over tens of millions of Americans, impoverishing and even paralyzing us at times.

Throughout the Bible, all the way to the book of Revelation, we are told that there is a proper sense in which we are to fear, or reverence, God. On the other hand, Jesus' followers have been delivered from the enslaving fear of death and what awaits us in the afterlife (Heb. 2:14–15). Those who have God as their Father need not be controlled by anxieties or fears. As Paul reminded his readers in Rome, "You did not receive the spirit of slavery to fall back into fear, but you have received the Spirit of adoption as sons, by whom we cry, 'Abba! Father!'" (Rom. 8:15). As Jesus' followers contemplate the day of judgment and the afterlife to follow, we need not fear punishment, but instead we can be confident in God's perfect love for us (1 John 4:17–18).

In heaven, then, as we enjoy the perfect care and provision of God our Father, there would seem to be nothing to worry about. Living in the perfect environment and loving relationships, for which God has designed us, it appears that there will be no more panic attacks, no more concerns with being socially humiliated, and no more irrational fears or avoidance of things we now perceive as threatening or dangerous. No more restless irritation and edginess. No more obsessing over negative, anxiety-causing thoughts. In heaven we won't catastrophize that the worst will happen. Instead, the God of peace (Rom. 15:33) will fill us with all peace (Rom. 15:13). After all, God's kingdom is characterized by righteousness and peace and joy in the Holy Spirit (Rom. 14:17). Full, abundant life in heaven will be completely free of debilitating anxiety (John 10:10). Ahh.

## Struggles in This Life

Of course, anxiety is not the only problem we struggle with in this life. As I work on this chapter, I am seated as an observer in the waiting room of a Christian counseling center here in Canton, Ohio. It's a relaxed, home-like atmosphere with comfortable overstuffed chairs and sofas. The receptionist is friendly and welcomes me when I explain the idea behind my book. Christian music plays in the background. Clients arrive and are greeted by their counselors. Dozens of books are displayed, with a sign indicating they may be borrowed for two weeks. Free booklets on the end table address *When Fear Seems Overwhelming* and *When a Spouse Is Unfaithful*. This particular center employs eleven counselors, with a reduced fee schedule for the uninsured.

The list of services they provide here is a daunting reminder of things we struggle with in this life: abuse, addiction, attention deficit disorder, anger management, Asperger's Syndrome, anxiety, career/work issues, cutting, depression, divorce recovery, domestic violence, eating disorders, family issues, grief, hoarding, intimacy issues, marriage counseling, mood disorders, obsessive-compulsive disorders, panic disorders, parenting problems, post-traumatic stress disorder, sexual addiction and behavioral issues, stress management, and trauma, among others.

Depression is just one of these two dozen issues, but it affects nearly twenty million Americans. It comes in many varieties, from post-partum depression and seasonal affective disorder to major depression and persistent depressive disorder. If we haven't been there ourselves, we know people who have been. It's tough to get out of bed in the morning. You just want to stay under the covers and not face any draining human contact. Maybe you miss some days at work. You don't feel much like eating and you may lose weight. Nothing seems fun anymore. Friends notice something is wrong. You're tired all the time and can't sleep well at night. Everything feels impossible, and you have no hope that things will ever change or get better. Ugh.

Lately I've been reading through the book of Psalms, and it's startling just how often the writers describe down times in their lives. Psalm 13:2 asks, "How long must I wrestle with my thoughts and every day have sorrow in my heart?" Psalm 31:9–10 says, "My eyes grow weak with sorrow, my soul and my body with grief. My life is consumed by anguish and my years by groaning; my strength fails because of my affliction, and my bones grow weak." Imagine a life consumed by sorrow, grief, anguish, and groaning. Serious depression. That's a tough way to live.

Psalm 88 describes rock bottom: "Day and night I cry out to you. . . . I am overwhelmed with troubles and my life draws near to death. . . . You have put me in the lowest pit, in the darkest depths. . . . I am confined and cannot escape; my eyes are dim with grief. . . . From my youth I have suffered and been close to death; I have borne your terrors and am in despair. . . . You have taken from me friend and neighbor—darkness is my closest friend." Or, as the Contemporary English Version concludes this gloomy psalm, "darkness is my only companion."

Of course there is hope for many who suffer from depression. Medication, counseling, exercise, and crying out to God in prayer (a common approach in the Psalms) often bring a measure of relief. But many people live with depression for most of their earthly years. Isaiah 53:3 describes the suffering servant, identified in the New Testament as Jesus Christ, as "a man of suffering, and familiar with pain" or a man of sorrows, and acquainted with grief. After narrating the afflictions, hardships, and sleepless nights he endured, the apostle Paul expresses in 2 Corinthians 6:10 how he was sorrowful, yet always rejoicing.

While sorrow and joy are mixed in different proportions during our earthly lives, in heaven it will be all joy with no sorrow. We are told that God's kingdom is marked by joy in the Holy Spirit (Rom. 14:17). Those who are good and faithful servants will be invited to "come and share your master's happiness" (Matt. 25:21, 23). In the new heaven and the new earth God "will wipe away every tear from their eyes. There will be no more death or mourning or crying or pain" (Rev. 21:4). Imagine life for all of God's people with no more sadness, melancholy, or blues.

In contrast to the darkness of depression in this life, we are told that in the heavenly life to come, "there will be no more night" because "the Lord God will give them light" (Rev. 22:5). Isaiah 35:10 and 51:11 both foretell how "those the LORD has rescued will return. They will enter Zion with singing; everlasting joy will crown their heads. Gladness and joy will overtake them, and sorrow and sighing will flee away." Sorrow and sighing will be replaced with gladness and glee! The promise of eternal life free from depression is one of the ways that "the God of hope fill[s] you with all joy and peace as you trust in him, so that you may overflow with hope by the power of the Holy Spirit" (Rom. 15:13). As I close my laptop and prepare to exit this local Christian counseling center, I find hope for myself and all of God's people, knowing that there will be no downheartedness, dejection, or despair in heaven, but instead joy forevermore!

## Troubles at Work

While anxiety and depression are among our most frequent personal issues in this life, we can be equally troubled by relational disturbances in our workplaces. There are different theories about work in heaven. Some say that in heaven we will totally cease from any sort of labor. In their interpretation of Hebrews 4:1–11, heaven will be one long Sabbath rest for God's people. Others say that work is part of God's good plan for people, in this life and the life to come. They note that Adam was assigned to work and keep the garden right from the beginning (Gen. 2:15), though when sin entered the scene, work became burdensome (Gen. 3:17–19). So, maybe in heaven we'll still have work to do, but it will be all delight and no drudgery, bringing us fulfillment in serving God (Rev. 7:15). What we know for sure is that all the activities in heaven, including any forms of work there, will not be tainted by anything accursed (Rev. 22:3).

Lots of people love their work and they love their boss. But, on the flip side, employment gurus tell us that the number one reason people quit their jobs is an unhealthy relationship with their boss. Bosses can be so weak or distant that they fail to support you in your job. Or they can blame every problem on you, while taking credit for the good work you've done. Worse yet, they can be intrusive, controlling bullies. Peter knew all about good employees who suffered under unjust bosses (1 Pet. 2:18–20). But he also knew that ultimately God's people have Jesus as their chief Shepherd (1 Pet. 5:4) and that they will enjoy "an inheritance that is imperishable, undefiled, and unfading, kept in heaven for you" (1 Pet. 1:4). No one in heaven will have to put up with a boss who is a jerk because heaven is where "the kingdom of the world has become the kingdom of our Lord and of his Christ, and he shall reign forever and ever" (Rev. 11:15). It will be pure pleasure to live under the reign of the perfect king Jesus!

Of course, workplace problems aren't limited to issues with the boss. The euphemism of "leaving due to personality conflicts" is usually just a polite way of saying that our relationships with fellow workers became so strained that we preferred to quit the job than continue to be around those people. Or they quit to get away from us. I've seen it on construction crews and I've seen it in university departments. But I won't see it in heaven. There everyone will be made perfect (Heb. 12:22–23). No one in heaven will be impossible to be around, including me! Joni Eareckson Tada says, "The best thing about heaven will be a pure heart no longer weighed down by sin and selfishness. . . . Glorified bodies? Hey, bring it on. But a pure, glorified heart? *That's* the best!"[1]

## Family Issues

While conflictual work relationships can be hard, dysfunctional marriage and family relations can be even worse. Like the nursery rhyme about the little girl who had a little curl right in the middle of her forehead, when marriages are good they are very, very good, but when they are bad they are horrid. Some people are married to their best friend and they're loving life together. But for other people, marriage is their hardest relationship on earth. In the U.S. somewhere in the neighborhood of four in ten marriages are so bad that they end in divorce. And of the marriages that remain intact, all too many are filled with headaches and heartaches. Unhappy marriages and divorces take a toll not just on the spouses but also on any children who may be involved. Jesus taught that divorce is caused by our hardheartedness, but this was not God's original design for marriage. God's plan was, and is, for the husband and wife to live together as one (Mark 10:2–12).

Thankfully the pain of broken homes will no longer exist in heaven, where there will be neither marriage nor divorce (Matt. 22:30). In heaven we'll never be devastated by a spouse who cheats on us. We'll never shrivel up emotionally in a cold, loveless marriage. We'll never be wronged or blamed unfairly by our spouse. There will be no more frustrating unresolved arguments, playing out the same tape over and over again. No more shattered dreams that we

---

1   Joni Eareckson Tada, *A Place of Healing: Wrestling with the Mysteries of Suffering, Pain, and God's Sovereignty* (Colorado Springs, CO: David C. Cook, 2010), 168. Italics in the original.

won't live happily ever after with Mr. Wonderful or Mrs. Right. No more lawyers' fees to divide the property and reach a settlement. No more lonely dinners for one. No more feeling unwanted and having everyone look at you with pity. No more pretending everything's okay when it's not.

No more awkwardness or worries when your ex has the kids for the weekend. No more pain of "being replaced" by a second spouse. In heaven no one will call you names, put you down, play mind games that make you think you're crazy, or otherwise make you feel bad about yourself. Again we're reminded that a big reason heaven will be heavenly is because of what is *not there*.

And that includes not only marital strife but all the other unhealthy family patterns we endure in this life. Even when a couple stays together for life, the family can still be miles away from what God intended for his kingdom. Due to the twisted dynamics of sin, sometimes a family member is wrongly marginalized or becomes a scapegoat for others' problems. Instead of affirming each other, families may demean each other. Family members may be unwilling to admit wrongdoing, apologize, or forgive each other.

I knew two brothers who worked the same shift in the same workplace and never spoke to each other for more than two decades. I still remember the year when one of my siblings bolted from the house before Christmas Eve and did not return, while another of my siblings set our parents' house on fire (it was extinguished). Even that didn't seem as bad as the Christmas when the f-bomb was dropped, followed by a physical altercation that ended with one branch of the family driving away in their mini-van.

Families can be places of sharing love and strong support, anchors that we cherish in our lives. But families can also be places of deep hurts and lasting scars. Promises may be broken and appropriate boundaries may be disrespected. Children can be defiant, and parents can be too lax or too heavy-handed. Communication can break down to the point where we no longer listen deeply or share meaningfully with each other. Physical, emotional, and sexual abuse may be tolerated or accepted as "normal" by the victims, perpetrators, and bystanders in families.

The Bible is all too realistic in portraying family issues. Within just the first portion of the book of Genesis, we read of Adam and Eve playing the blame game (Gen. 3), which is nothing compared to their first son Cain killing their second son Abel (Gen. 4). When Abraham and Sarah decide to use Hagar as a surrogate mother, it leads to a fractured family (Gen. 16), which again is eclipsed by Lot offering his virgin daughters to gang rapists before himself engaging in drunken incest with them (Gen. 19). Jacob swindles his brother Esau's birthright by lying to their dad with the help of their mom. Then Jacob runs away to live with his uncle Laban, who tricks Jacob into marrying his undesirable daughter, Leah, before throwing in a marriage to his desirable daughter, Rachel, in exchange for seven more years of labor (Gen. 27–29). Families here on earth can be really messed up, but in heaven God's family will be healthy and whole.

### Relationships in Heaven

We don't know exactly how relationships will work in heaven. On the one hand, we are told that in heaven there will be no more marriage (Matt. 22:30, Mark 12:25, Luke 20:34–35). On the other hand, we are also told that in heaven there will be people who are identifiably from every nation, tribe, people, and language (Rev. 5:9–10; 7:9–10). We will remain distinct individuals (Matt. 8:11; Luke 20:37–38), with unique characteristics that we bring to our relationships.

We are also told that God has graciously allowed his people to become partakers of the divine nature (2 Pet. 1:4), so that in the afterlife God's children will be like God himself (1 John 3:2). That will change everything about our relationships! Since God is faithful, good, and holy, we can safely assume that our relationships in heaven will be marked by faithfulness, goodness, and holiness. Since God is just, loving, and truthful, we can also assume that our relationships in heaven will be marked by justice, love, and truthfulness. Then Jesus' prayer will be answered, that his people will be one, in the same way that he and the Father are one — distinct persons who exist, along with the Spirit, in relationships of perfect unity, harmony, and love (John 17:21–23).

Imagine no more broken promises in marriage. No more scheming or backstabbing at work. No more hurtful words or actions in the family. No more hating a spouse or wishing someone else dead. No more cheating to get ahead or shading the truth to make oneself look better at the job. No more slipping into unhealthy patterns with family members. No more selfishly looking out for number one. Instead, everyone will always keep their word and do what is good and holy. Everyone will act justly and love others. We are right when we say "that will be heaven."

My wife and I both earned graduate degrees in clinical psychology and both of us have done our share of counseling, paid and unpaid. But in heaven there will be no more need to counsel the abused. No need to confront or to support the addicted. No more drugs to help with ADHD. No more anger management groups. No more cutting or self-harm. No more domestic violence. No more marriage counseling or divorce adjustment. No more eating disorders, though there are indications that there will be eating in heaven (Matt. 8:11; Mark 14:25; Luke 13:29). No more family counseling or parenting consultations. No more problems with obsessions, compulsions, or panic disorders. No more porn or sexual perversion (1 Cor. 6:9–11; Rev. 21:8). No more PTSD or coping with trauma. No more need for any mental health professionals or services!

On the softer side, we won't need sleeping pills to stop our minds from whirring or our bodies from fidgeting. We won't need self-help books to guide us through life. We won't need Oprah, Dr. Phil, or others to expose people's life problems or provide advice. We won't ever worry about money again. We will no longer be concerned with what others think about us, and we won't spend a single minute crafting our self-presentations on social media. Instead, we will know ourselves to be completely loved by God (Rom. 1:7; 1 Thess. 1:4). We will rest secure in our identity as more than conquerors though him who loved us, confident that nothing in all creation will be able to separate us from God's love in Christ Jesus our Lord (Rom. 8:37–39).

## Derek Clark's Story

Derek Clark's father was put in a prison for the criminally insane. His abusive mother kept his brother and sister, but dropped off 5-year-old Derek at county social services. He spent the next thirteen years in the foster care system, always in trouble and labeled as "mentally handicapped." Though he felt forgotten and rejected by his family, he hoped to reunite with them. That dream was shattered when his older sister was murdered on Mother's Day, followed shortly by his foster brother and mentor being killed in an accident. Derek was filled with anger and determined he would hate God forever. He blamed God whenever anything bad happened.

Derek succeeded in business but his world was truly rocked when a friend's daughter nearly drowned in Derek's pool during a barbecue. Derek saw his friend trust God supernaturally in the midst of the crisis and then saw the girl miraculously spared. Derek cried out in thanks to God and began to see his own life through different lenses, realizing God had been with him at every point in his life. Derek reports going from feeling abandoned by God to feeling embraced by God, a story he shares as a motivational speaker and as an author.[2] While Derek's story is truly inspirational

---

2 Derek W. Clark, *I Will Never Give Up* (n.p.: Never Limit Your Life Publishing, 2008), and Derek W. Clark, *I Will Never Give Up on God Again* (n.p.: Never Limit Your Life Publishing, 2009).

and he has found a remarkable measure of healing in this life, he still has problems that will not be fully resolved until he is glorified in heaven (Rom. 8:17, 30).

Like Derek, in this life we all experience headaches and heartaches, whether it's struggling with anxiety or depression, problems with the boss or co-workers, or family issues. Many of us have simply accepted that human existence has always been tough and it will always be tough. But while it's true that this life will always have its struggles and pains, heaven will be completely pain-free (Rev. 21:4)! Looking forward to heaven gives God's people life-giving hope that there will come a time, an everlasting, never-ending time, when our hearts will never ache again.

*For Individual Reflection or Group Discussion*

1. What makes you anxious or gets you down? Imagine never feeling this way again, ever.

2. As you look back over all the jobs you've done, who or what has been especially tough at work for you? In light of Scripture, what is your understanding of work and rest in heaven?

3. Contrast challenges in your family life now with what we know about relationships in heaven.

4. How can you encourage someone in your life who is like Derek Clark, with big life obstacles?

## Interview with Greg Jurica

**Brief Bio:** Greg is a professional therapist who specializes in counseling persons with addiction. I've been in a marriage group with Greg, who is also my neighbor and faithful servant at church.

*What has been the hardest thing about your experience on earth as a counselor?*

My greatest challenge so far has been reconciling my Christ-centered beliefs and God-worldview with the many tenets of secular psychology. There is some congruence; other times there is not. I personally look to Scripture as the inerrant source for grace and healing, whereas many of my colleagues and clients do not. But what a wonderful opportunity to witness, to hear stories and provide hope and healing, and to let my life speak for God's purpose. I further struggle with seeing depravity, evil, and the overall suffering of the human condition. It requires much prayer and seeking of Christ, and also good supervision to process the things I encounter in the world of mental health and alcohol/drug treatment. I've been given a gift and the skills to work with those who are suffering. I rely on God's strength, courage, and perspective to guide me as a therapist.

*From your perspective as a counselor, what do you most look forward to in heaven?*

I most look forward to the end of suffering, pain, and tears. I work with so many people who have hurting souls, bodies, and mental/emotional states. And, like most, I have also suffered in my personal life. Heaven brings us a new and beautiful life of unending worship, alongside brothers and sisters, as one with our Creator and Savior.

*Share a time when, as a counselor, you had at least a "glimpse of heaven on earth."*

I consider any success in therapy or even any small motivation for change as a "glimpse of heaven on earth." I do not take this type of glimpse lightly. When I witness change or even strong motivation for change in a sufferer, I view this as a gift from God. Any relief or anything good comes from him (James 1:17). I get a glimpse of heaven when young, pregnant, opiate-addicted women, with unborn lives at stake, have the courage to seek treatment—knowing the dangers of IV drug use and related withdrawal. God has entrusted me with their care.

### Interview with Marsha Raymond

**Brief Bio:** Marsha is a counselor who helps women process through their pregnancy options and make informed decisions. She inspires me and others at our church to put our faith into action.

*What has been the hardest thing about your experience on earth as a pregnancy counselor?*

The hardest thing for me, personally, is when I meet with a client who has a particularly hard life-story or circumstances. Hearing these young women speak of the terrible things they have experienced is heart-breaking. One client told me that her father, a heroin addict, used to sell her to his friends for money. At 13 years old, she was being prostituted by her own father. It is so hard to hear these stories about how evil our world truly is. My life often seems like a bubble of safety and happiness, in comparison.

*From your perspective as a counselor, what do you most look forward to in heaven?*

I most look forward to the promise in Revelation 21:4 that there will be no more tears, death, mourning, crying, or pain. All of the trials and tribulations that my clients go through on earth; their lack of an earthly father who loves them, their painful pasts, their brokenness, will be no more. All things will be new, and good, and perfect. That's part of why I love sharing the gospel with them — it offers an eternity that is beyond anything most of them have experienced on earth. And knowing Jesus, in the meantime, can make a huge difference in their lives here as well!

*Share a time when, as a counselor, you had at least a "glimpse of heaven on earth."*

The same client whom I mentioned above poured her heart out to me — including her father's abuse, her own struggles with drugs and the law, the fact that her children had been taken away from her, a lifetime that seemed to be without meaning. She cried out for help and I told her about Jesus. The air in the room was thick as she listened, her eyes lighting up as I spoke. She heard the gospel with open and ready ears. And she received Christ right there in the counseling room. I feel that seeing her "get it," joyfully accepting that she was forgiven, was a "glimpse of heaven on earth." I saw God's mighty power, splendor, and grace displayed all in one defining moment. Everything Satan had intended to harm her with, and hurt her by, Christ overcame. It was a powerful moment and I will never forget her, or what I saw God do in her life.

# 4

## Security Issues: No More Prisons, Passwords, or Protecting Ourselves

TODAY I DECIDED TO PAY A FRIENDLY VISIT to the Stark County Jail. The painted brick walls and connected institutional chairs are much less inviting than the overstuffed furniture I enjoyed at the Christian counseling center as I worked on the previous chapter. On my way in to the building I saw several prisoners in their orange jump suits, attended by officers in blue uniforms. Now I'm seated with five women who are waiting to see their loved ones behind bars. Judge Judy blares from the TV mounted on the wall, and the women toggle between watching the show, chatting with each other, and fiddling with their cell phones. A sign indicates that on the other side of the locked door, no cell phones are permitted in the visiting room. This isn't the kind of place you come to for a good time. It has a grim, gloomy feel to it.

The Stark County Jail is located within a few hundred yards of residential homes and most of the neighbors don't worry too much about being so near to the inmates. The jail holds mostly people who have been convicted of minor charges. The pastor at our former church used to jog regularly right along the border of the jail grounds. It's a different story near other correctional facilities.

Just this week two murderers escaped from a maximum security penitentiary in New York, and everyone within a thirty-mile radius was on high alert. One of the escapees had been charged with rape and was incarcerated for kidnapping, killing, and dismembering his former boss. People who lived there were terrified. This same week a local man from Akron, Ohio, was convicted of killing his ex-girlfriend's parents with a sledgehammer. There are too many stories like this.

Just after college, my wife did an internship in a state penitentiary, working with criminally insane men (a great prelude to marrying me!). As she tells it, most of them seemed like nice guys. They served her tea and made sure to pull out the chair for her before the group sessions. They enjoyed many friendly conversations about current events. She was shocked to learn that one of these "nice men" was convicted of killing his wife because she changed the channel on the TV. By the end of her internship, Sue wondered if she could fully trust anyone.

Murderers pose a lethal threat, and our society has deemed it best to lock them away (or in rare cases, execute them). Most people agree that we need prisons in this life. In heaven we won't need prisons because no one there will do wrong. Specifically, we are told that there will be no people who are murderers, liars, or sexually immoral in heaven (Rev. 21:8; 22:15). Of course, by God's standards, we are all guilty of forms of murder and adultery (Matt. 5:21–30). But God will so transform his people in heaven that no one will ever wrong anyone else again. Our security will never be threatened in heaven. We will finally experience a true and complete safety!

### No More Bad Guys

The U.S. Department of Justice reports that the rate of sexual assault has declined in the past two decades. That's a good thing. Still, there are around a quarter million Americans, age 12 or older, who are victimized by rape and sexual assault each year. In the U.S. someone is sexually assaulted every two minutes, the time it takes to read this page. That's a hideous, horrific thing. Sexual assault is a realistic fear that lurks in the mind of nearly every woman. A recent survey found that 25% of college women experienced unwanted sexual contact during their years as undergraduate students. That's 25% too many. It should be zero.

My wife's birthday is in two weeks and I asked her how she'd like to celebrate it. She wants to wait until two days after her birthday and go to the state fair with me and our daughters. The evening of her actual birthday she's tentatively penciled in going to a women's self-defense class at the YMCA. I'm not sure if she'll do it or not, but it's a screwed-up world when a woman thinks about spending the evening of her birthday at a self-defense class.

In heaven no one will ever worry about being sexually assaulted. There will be no more need for self-defense classes in karate or kick boxing. No more carrying mace or pepper spray. No more worrying about our daughters, mothers, and friends. No more warning our kids about strangers or explaining the difference between "good touch" and "bad touch." No more public education campaigns, fraternity awareness programs, or take-back-the-night marches. There won't be even a hint of sexual harassment, including the subtle behaviors, gestures, and comments that make us uncomfortable (Rev. 21:8, 27; 22:15). It's almost hard for us to imagine. It's heaven!

With no wrongdoers in heaven, there will also be no need for the twelve thousand local police departments now operating in the U.S. No drug investigations, bomb threats, or SWAT teams. No detectives interrogating suspects, interviewing witnesses, or testifying in court. No patrol officers on foot or in cruisers to keep the streets safe. No more uniforms, nightsticks, or Tasers. Not even any more speeding tickets or traffic violations! Police are such a big part of our lives, including dozens of TV crime shows, that it's hard to imagine a world without them. As I drive away from the Stark County Jail, I hunger for life in heaven, free of prisons and police.

## No More War

Taken to the international level, there will be no more military in heaven. No more army with tanks, self-propelled guns, or rocket projectors on the ground. No more navy and coast guard with aircraft carriers, submarines, or mine warfare on the water. No more air force with F-22 Raptors, F-35 Lightning IIs, or attack helicopters in the sky. No more marines with howitzers, grenade launchers, or M16 rifles anywhere. No more folded flags handed out at funerals, and no more of my veteran friends haunted by nightmares and other after-effects of PTSD. News of war and its suffering weighs us all down with sadness, a sadness that will be lifted in heaven.

If war is understood as an active conflict in which at least a thousand people die, it is estimated that the world has been at war for more than 90% of recorded human history, with more than one hundred million people killed just in the twentieth century. Nearly $2 trillion goes to military spending every year worldwide, but there will be no need for that in heaven. The prophets Isaiah (2:4) and Micah (4:3) both look forward to a time when people "will beat their swords into plowshares and their spears into pruning hooks. Nation will not take up sword against nation, nor will they train for war anymore." The deep human longing to be free from war will be fulfilled!

There will be no more international conflicts in heaven because everyone there will enjoy a common citizenship with a common savior, the Lord Jesus Christ (Phil. 3:20). All believers will be "fellow citizens with God's people and also members of his household" (Eph. 2:19). John's vision of heaven features "a great multitude that no one could count, from every nation, tribe, people and language, standing before the throne and before the Lamb" (Rev. 7:9). And rather than wearing national military uniforms and holding weapons in their hands, John tells us "they were wearing white robes and were holding palm branches in their hands" (Rev. 7:9). What a beautiful picture of heavenly shalom: harmonious peace under the reign of the Prince of Peace!

## No More Stealing

Of course, peace and security issues go beyond prisons, police, and the military to the everyday routines most of us hardly notice. We lock up our windows and doors to keep intruders out of our cars and homes. We close our garages and chain up our bikes to discourage theft. We install security cameras to monitor and record access to areas where stealing is likely. My daughter just had her cell phone stolen, which is a real pain in the neck. In the United States alone, more than one and a half million cell phones are stolen every year, not to mention more than $10 billion in alcohol, clothing, cosmetics, electronics, and other items that are shoplifted from stores in the U.S. annually. I was surprised to learn how often meats are stolen from supermarkets. Just tuck that steak under your jacket and saunter on out the door. Or at a shoe store, walk in wearing flip flops and walk right by the register in a new pair of Adidases or Nikes. Happens all the time.

Physical theft has been around forever but cyber theft is the newest way to steal. With the help of an undercover agent using an assumed name, cyber cops recently broke up an international cybercrime syndicate known as carder.su. This organization, whose Russian leaders are still at large, included nearly eight thousand cyber criminals who victimized hundreds of thousands of Americans to the tune of $50 million in financial fraud. When federal agents raided the organization, they recovered more than two hundred thousand stolen credit and debit card numbers. But that's the tip of the iceberg.

Losses from credit card and debit card fraud total more than $10 billion annually. That may explain why, according to some surveys, cyber fraud is now the number one fear of Americans, outstripping even concerns with terrorism and health. People worry all the time about having their credit card numbers, social security numbers, and bank/investment numbers stolen. People also worry that data compromises from the health-care, government, education, and retail sectors may result in identity theft, which now costs people more than all other types of stealing (burglary, motor vehicle, and other property theft) combined. The whole world of cyber theft is so complicated that I try just not to think about it. But denial only lasts until you're victimized. Last month my wife had an unauthorized charge and had to cancel a credit card.

None of that in heaven. No credit cards with annoying security numbers on the back. No bank or investment account numbers to keep track of. No passwords to invent, forget, and retrieve. My wife and I try (unsuccessfully!) to keep our online accounts to a minimum, but I just added them up and we have seventy, none of which are supposed to have the same username or password. Sometimes I wonder how important it is to keep our Chipotle "account" secure, but I'm sure there must be a reason to have yet one more username and password added to the clutter of our lives. I look forward, in heaven, to the relief of not always feeling we have to be on guard.

In the midst of all our concerns with stealing, it is jolting to consider Jesus' words to his followers in Matthew 6:19–20: "Do not store up for yourselves treasures on earth . . . where thieves break in and steal. But store up for yourselves treasures in heaven . . . where thieves do not break in and steal." I can't wait for that day! Among the wrongdoers who won't inherit the kingdom of God, Paul specifically mentions thieves (1 Cor. 6:10). Of course, if you're like me, you've stolen at some time in your life, but the only people in heaven will be those who have had their stealing and all their other sins washed away in Jesus' name (1 Cor. 6:11).

## Our Deep Desire to Be Safe and Secure

To increase our security and deal with our fears, we hire all sorts of people. Unarmed security guards can be found at the entrances to many buildings. The TSA employs roughly fifty thousand officers to screen people and their luggage at the entry points of airports. Then there are armed security officers who deal with higher-risk situations such as transporting valuables in Brinks trucks. The rich and famous even employ bodyguards to deter threats from stalkers and annoyances from paparazzi when their clients head out to eat, shop, or attend awards ceremonies. Funny how I've never required a bouncer to accompany me anywhere. Hmm. Anyway, in this life, security is big business. And so is insurance, as we try to protect ourselves against losses. Most people in the U.S. seem to have health insurance, home or renter insurance, as well as car insurance. Insurance policies can cover just about anything imaginable—from the more common life insurance and disability insurance to the less common alien abduction insurance and policies to cover werewolf, vampire, and zombie attacks! While we chuckle at Proctor & Gamble taking out a million-dollar insurance policy on the famous three-foot-long locks of their spokesman, Pittsburgh Steelers safety Troy Polamalu, our interest in insurance may reflect something deeper.

Psychologist Abraham Maslow's famous hierarchy of human needs suggests that right after physiological needs such as air, water, and food, humans' next most basic needs are for safety and security. Perhaps that explains why God promised the Israelites that if they carefully obeyed his laws, they would be able to eat all the food they wanted, and they would live in the Promised Land in safety (Lev. 25:18–19; 26:5–6). Like the Psalmist, many of us call out to God in prayer, asking him to keep us safe from wicked people who would do us harm (Pss. 140:4; 141:9).

We especially want to keep our children safe and secure. Put negatively, many of us have a deep fear that our kids will be injured, harmed, or die. It's why we place babies on their backs to sleep. It's why we require kids to ride in car seats. It's why we have them take swim lessons and instruct them about fire safety. It's why we have anti-bullying policies and require teens to take drivers' education before they get their licenses. It's why we have students go through lockdown drills at school—practicing being quiet and still, but simultaneously prepared to throw objects at intruders who get into the room. It's one of the reasons we're outraged when there is a school shooting, which reminds us that, try as we may, we cannot truly guarantee our kids' safety.

Fences, secure doors, and metal detectors might help, but they cannot always stop determined shooters. Our security plans are imperfect, people end up propping doors open, and those who are resolved to kill can find ways around our prevention efforts. When we kiss our kids goodbye and send them off with their oversized backpacks, we want to know they're safe and secure, but the scary reality is there are things beyond our control. As child psychologist Rahil Briggs said in the wake of the Sandy Hook Elementary School shootings, "Children are relatively helpless and they rely on us to help make their world safe. It's especially heartbreaking when we can't."[1] Even in an idyllic rural Amish setting, unthinkable violence can take place in a school building. Just this week a gunman killed nine students in an Oregon community college. We wonder if we're safe anywhere.

Besides seeking physical safety, humans also seek emotional safety. In our relationships we often ask ourselves, *Will they accept me? Do they like me? Will they hurt me? Will I fail them?* Through a process that scientists call neuroception, our minds and bodies are constantly determining whether our situation is safe, dangerous, or life-threatening. When we feel safe, our voices and our faces are physically energized to communicate emotional nuance and we are most likely to engage others socially. When we sense a danger, especially something life-threatening, our social engagement capacities essentially go dark and other systems light up.

People who are exposed to war, neglect, abuse, or trauma may be more likely to be emotionally guarded, self-protective, and self-reliant. My wife is a CASA/Guardian Ad Litem for kids who are neglected and abused. She sees that guarded look and self-protective behavior all the time. Too many children's life experiences have taught them to be afraid. But imagine every kid in heaven flourishing and feeling emotionally safe because their environment and relationships are characterized by steady, unwavering love and acceptance. We can and must work on increasing people's physical and emotional safety on earth, but true, lasting security is found in heaven.

---

1   Bonnie Rochman, "Trying to Make Sense of Tragedy: Why the Sandy Hook Shooting Is So Painful for All of Us," *Time,* Dec. 17, 2012.

## Paul's Perspective on Heaven

Consider these highlights from Paul's life as an apostle:

> Five times I received from the Jews the forty lashes minus one. Three times I was beaten with rods, once I was pelted with stones, three times I was shipwrecked, I spent a night and a day in the open sea, I have been constantly on the move. I have been in danger from rivers, in danger from bandits, in danger from my fellow Jews, in danger from Gentiles; in danger in the city, in danger in the country, in danger at sea; and in danger from false believers. I have labored and toiled and have often gone without sleep; I have known hunger and thirst and have often gone without food; I have been cold and naked. (2 Cor. 11:24–27)

And yet Paul could say, in the same letter to the Corinthians, that he did not lose heart, "for our light and momentary troubles are achieving for us an eternal glory that far outweighs them all. So we fix our eyes not on what is seen, but on what is unseen, since what is seen is temporary, but what is unseen is eternal" (2 Cor. 4:17–18).

Mentally, Paul pulls out a balance of scales. In the pan on the left side he puts all that he has suffered for the sake of Christ, which turns out to be a huge, heaping pile. But in the pan on the right side he puts the glory that he will enjoy forever in heaven, and he finds that it far outweighs anything he's had to endure on earth. The scale goes crashing down on the right side of eternal glory in heaven. As Paul puts it, "I consider that our present sufferings are not worth comparing with the glory that will be revealed in us" (Rom. 8:18). It's no contest. For God's people, weighty glory in heaven dwarfs our comparatively light sufferings on earth.

## Earthly Suffering and Heavenly Joy

Think of Stephen (Acts 7) and Christian martyrs in the early, medieval, and modern church. Ignatius was fed to the lions at the beginning of the second century. His view of the afterlife inspired him to live out his words: "Let the crowds of wild beasts; let tearings, breaking, and dislocations of bones; let cutting off of members; let shatterings of the whole body; and let all the dreadful torments of the devil come upon me: only let me attain to Jesus Christ."[2] In the fifteenth century, before he was burned at the stake, the martyr Jan Hus reportedly lifted his eyes to heaven and said, "I do commend into Thy hands, O Lord Jesus Christ, my spirit which Thou has redeemed." Hus also said, in the martyr spirit, that "it is better to die well than to live badly."[3]

In the twentieth century, several Ecuadorian missionaries were killed by Auca Indians (now known as the Waodani or Huaorani people), with whom they were trying to make friendly contact. One of them, Jim Elliot, famously summed up his primary allegiance to God's heavenly kingdom in the following entry in his personal journal on October 28, 1949. "One of the great blessings of heaven is the appreciation of heaven on earth—Ephesian truth. He is no fool who gives what he cannot keep to gain that which he cannot lose."[4] Think about that. Martyrs take Jesus at his word when he says, "Whoever loses their life for my sake will find it" (Matt. 10:39).

Christian martyrs draw dramatic attention to a conviction that all Christians should share—that earthly death is not really the end of life. That is one of the reasons that, historically, martyred and

---

2  "The Epistle of Ignatius to the Romans," in Alexander Roberts and James Donaldson, eds., *The Ante-Nicene Fathers,* vol. 1 (New York: Charles Scribner's Sons, 1903), 76.

3  Thomas A. Fudge, *Jan Hus: Religious Reform and Social Revolution in Bohemia* (New York: I. B. Tauris, 2010), 134.

4  Elisabeth Elliot, ed., *The Journals of Jim Elliot* (Old Tappan, NJ: Revell, 1978), 174.

non-martyred Christians were celebrated and remembered not on the day of their earthly birth but on the day of their earthly death, or their "birth into heaven." Just before he was hung for his role in the plot to assassinate Hitler, Lutheran pastor and theologian Dietrich Bonhoeffer gave voice to the Christian belief that "This is the end. . . . For me, the beginning of life."[5]

The Greek word *martus* can also be translated as "witness." Martyrs are powerful witnesses to the paradox noted by John Saward that, "by the mysterious workings of God's providence, those men [and women] in the history of the Church who have attended most to the things above have done most to transform things here below."[6] Christian martyrs are a witness to the truth that, "if only for this life we have hope in Christ, we are of all people most to be pitied" (1 Cor. 15:19). But martyrs also know that "the kingdom of heaven is like treasure hidden in a field. When a man found it, he hid it again, and then in his joy went and sold all he had and bought that field" (Matt. 13:44). Martyrs are inspiring witnesses that "to live is Christ and to die is gain" (Phil. 1:21).

## God's Provision for Our Deepest Needs

Deep inside of us we long for safety and security. Prisons, police, and pepper spray are all meant to protect us. Programs to prevent identity theft, policies against catastrophic loss, and protocols for school lockdowns are intended to keep us safe. Security is a basic human need. It's why we consider spending a birthday at a self-defense class. It's why we have the army, navy, air force, and marines. It's why we have locks on our windows, doors, and computer accounts. It's why we may be emotionally guarded in our relationships. The U.S. gov-

---

5   Eric Metaxas, *Bonhoeffer: Pastor, Martyr, Prophet, Spy* (Nashville, TN: Thomas Nelson, 2010), 517.

6   John Saward, *Sweet and Blessed Country: The Christian Hope for Heaven* (New York: Oxford University Press, 2005), 53.

ernment provides "social security" to help people feel more secure about their retirement years. But aside from all these measures we take to increase our security on earth, God's people are called to look to him and to the afterlife, where we will experience ultimate, never-ending "social security" from God's hand.

In Psalm 16, King David puts it this way:

> Keep me safe, my God, for in you I take refuge. . . . LORD, you alone are my portion and my cup; you make my lot secure. . . . I keep my eyes always on the LORD. With him at my right hand, I will not be shaken. Therefore my heart is glad and my tongue rejoices; my body also will rest secure, because you will not abandon me to the realm of the dead, nor will you let your faithful one see decay. You make known to me the path of life; you will fill me with joy in your presence, with eternal pleasures at your right hand.

David rests secure with his eyes on the Lord. He anticipates the joy and eternal pleasures he will experience in God's presence because he trusts in God's provision for him in the afterlife.

The author of Hebrews also speaks of our God-given hope "as an anchor for the soul, firm and secure" (6:19), which is focused on the heavenly sanctuary, "where our forerunner, Jesus, has entered on our behalf" (6:20). The hope of heaven is an anchor for the souls of God's people, providing us with stability and security in the midst of life's uncertainties. In this earthly life we can join David in trusting that "it is God who arms me with strength and keeps my way secure" (2 Sam. 22:33; Ps. 18:32). The bad news is that in this life most of us experience times of insecurity, some more than others, but the great news for all of God's people is found in heaven, where we "will live securely" (Mic. 5:4). What a day that will be!

*For Individual Reflection or Group Discussion*

1. What does it mean to you personally that there will be no more murder, no more lying/deceit, and no more impurity/immorality in heaven (Rev. 21:8; 21:27; 22:15)? When you recognize how we are all guilty of forms of murder and adultery (Matt. 5:21–30), how do you react?

2. How have you been touched, directly or indirectly, by war and/or by theft? When you consider that there will be no more war or theft in heaven, what is your response?

3. From the sections on Paul and the martyrs, which quote or story did you find most inspiring? Share an area of your life that you need to approach from a more heavenly perspective.

4. What do you look to here on earth to keep you safe and secure (your job, money, police, locks, weapons, etc.)? Compare these sources of security with God and his heavenly kingdom.

## Interview with Denny Thornton

**Brief Bio:** Denny served as a hospital corpsman, second class, from 1968 to 1972, including time in Vietnam. I've been privileged to spend six years with Denny in a men's Bible study at church.

*What was the hardest thing about your experience on earth in the military?*

The hardest thing that I had to deal with during my time in the navy was the sights, sounds, and suffering of sailors and marines killed or wounded in Vietnam. At the Naval Medical Center in Bethesda, Maryland, we used to go out to Andrews Air Force base with buses and ambulances and unload the cargo bays from jets, which were full of the most severely and profoundly injured marines and naval personnel. When I was in Vietnam, civilian casualties and the impact of the war on them was heartbreaking. I had to harden myself to what I was seeing and doing and set aside emotion, and sometimes fear, because it was the only way that I could perform my duties. When I see the commercials on TV for the Wounded Warrior Project I have to look away or find some way to divert my thoughts from those days and the scenes that are still in my mind's eye.

*From your perspective as a military veteran, what do you most look forward to in heaven?*

I look forward to the Isaiah 2:4 scenario for the kingdom which is to come. A heaven where conflict and injury and death are not only absent but are as far removed from our memory as the east is from the west. When I see the Wounded Warrior Project commercial featuring the man in a persistent vegetative state, it just tears me apart to see how devastated and emotional his wife is and how it affects his child. I have seen too many men like him. Someday we will meet in heaven and he will be in a new whole body and we will dance together.

*Share a time when, in your military role, you had at least a "glimpse of heaven on earth."*

I'm ashamed to say that at that point in my life I didn't give much consideration to either heaven or hell. I was once stationed on the island of Guam. I had been snorkeling inside of the reef area and I got way too far out. Suddenly I realized I was being carried out to sea by the tide. Not being a strong swimmer I was in trouble and was probably going to die. But God had a plan for me. He knew that I had not accepted his son yet. An inner voice told me to swim, and so I did. The mercy shown to me that day was a glimpse of God's grace and forgiveness and how even as sinners we can approach God and heaven through his son. He truly is a God of second chances.

### Interview with Sherry Shindle

**Brief Bio:** Sherry served for three years in the U.S. Army in Fort Knox, Kentucky, and Ansbach, Germany. She sings on our worship team, and her face glows visibly from anywhere in the church.

*What was the hardest thing about your experience on earth in the military?*

The hardest thing for me was maintaining my beliefs and Christian way of life in the military environment, which wasn't always friendly to my faith. My first husband decided I should join him in the military in an effort to gain even more control over me (in an abusive marriage). By God's grace, it worked out the other way, with my time in the army providing me with the protection and the courage to live my life in a much more healthy way.

*From your perspective as a military veteran, what do you most look forward to in heaven?*

I look forward to the fact that we won't need a military in heaven, and that all who are in heaven will be made whole. While my military experience (no combat) was mostly positive, it was hard for me when our son served in the military, including more than a year in Afghanistan. He saw so many sacrifices people made there, sacrifices that we won't have to make in heaven, where instead we will celebrate the sacrifice of Jesus for us (Rev. 5:9–12).

*Share a time when, in your military role, you had at least a "glimpse of heaven on earth."*

As I mentioned earlier, God used the army to take me from a place of struggle to a place of peace, much like heaven will take us from our earthly struggles to a state of perfect peace. When I was in the army God brought people into my life who served as rescuers, which for me was like a little glimpse of Jesus, who rescues us from all that's wrong in our lives here on earth.

# 5

## Social Issues: No More Terrorism, Tear Gas, or Tsunamis

I WALK INTO THE DOWNTOWN LOBBY of Canton's Goodwill community campus. It's a nice facility, decorated with soothing colors and a professional feel. More importantly, it's a place where people receive all sorts of help with the woes of this world. The receptionist and marketing director welcome me when I explain what I'm doing with this book. I position myself in an unobtrusive spot, so as to not disturb the clients or the workers as they come and go.

Goodwill helps people overcome barriers to employment and other life challenges. My mom volunteers for a few hours every Monday morning in adult literacy classes. It's impressive. But the building where I'm seated goes way beyond Goodwill. It also houses more than a dozen non-profit organizations that collaborate in serving the community. Over the years I've been privileged to accompany college students from our "Faith in the World" class on tours of this facility.

### Navigating Local Problems

The first tour stop is the offices of Access Health Stark County. They help those of us who are uninsured, or need to sign up for Medicaid, or are lost in the health-care maze. But maybe my problem is that I need an expensive medication that I can't afford. Then I can make an appointment at the second tour stop: Prescription Assistance Network of Stark County. It's basically a charitable pharmacy that helps sustain the lives of thousands of vulnerable people. The third stop is the American Red Cross, which trains people in CPR, first aid, and lifeguarding, helps people in times of disaster, and serves as the largest supplier of blood in the U.S. These are three terrific organizations doing great things.

As amazing as these social services are, they won't be needed in heaven. No one in heaven will worry about navigating the health-care system, and no one there will require an expensive medication they can't afford. There will be no more need to administer first aid or rescue people with CPR. With God on the throne, we won't need any lifeguards perched on their chairs, ready to save. In heaven, "there will be no more death or mourning or crying or pain" (Rev. 21:4).

In heaven people will no longer have to give blood, platelets, or plasma or to keep each other alive. The blood that matters most in heaven is the blood Jesus shed on behalf of others. John describes Jesus as the one "who loves us and has freed us from our sins by his blood" (Rev. 1:5). In heaven God's people will sing about how worthy Jesus is, "because you were slain, and with your blood you purchased for God persons from every tribe and language and people and nation" (Rev. 5:9). No more worries about running low on type O blood or whether someone's Rh factor is positive or negative. Jesus' blood has already made everything right for his people in heaven.

After the three health care stops, we move further into the building to offices designed to serve mainly older people. Those who feel the work world has passed them by can use Mature Services for help with job training and placement. Those who are suffering memory loss or their families can stop in next door at the Alzheimer's Association for emotional support and practical resources. People with a loved one at the end of life can receive assistance from Community Hospice of Stark County, which helps keep the dying as comfortable as possible. I'm deeply thankful for these services that assist and honor the elderly. After all, the Bible says to "stand up in the presence of the aged, show respect for the elderly and revere your God" (Lev. 19:32).

Beyond that, the Bible also says, "precious in the sight of the LORD is the death of his faithful servants" (Ps. 116:15). God calls us to help the elderly in a respectful way, and it is precious to God when his faithful followers pass from this life to the next. My grandfather was a sort of hero and key role model for me. When he died at age 104, I grieved deeply. But I smile when I think of "Beepa" in heaven. Jesus said, "The righteous will shine like the sun in the kingdom of their Father" (Matt. 13:43). My heart soars as I picture my grandfather beaming and radiant!

While there are many more offices at Canton's Goodwill campus, we'll make just three more stops to wrap up our tour. The Stark County Hunger Task Force has a pantry where county residents can pick up essential foods every month. They also prepare "backpacks" of food on Fridays for kids who get free and reduced school lunches during the week. It makes me sad to think of all the children who go through life hungry. Of course, children need more than just food, which is why Big Brothers Big Sisters matches kids with a mentor to support them and help them succeed in life. Lastly, there's United Way 2-1-1, a three-digit phone line people can call 24/7 when they're not sure where to start. It's the catchall for help in our county.

I'm inspired by what these organizations do—feeding the hungry, loving children, and helping people just like Jesus did when he was on earth. But in heaven we won't have to combat these problems. There won't be any more hunger pangs (Rev. 21:4) when God's people "take their places at the feast with Abraham, Isaac and Jacob in the kingdom of heaven" (Matt. 8:11). There won't be any more unloved children. We won't need to call 2-1-1 for help in heaven. I walk out of the Goodwill building with gratitude and admiration for all the good that is done here, but also with anticipation of heaven's future bliss, when "God himself will be with them" (Rev. 21:3).

## Tackling Economic Issues

Local problems are challenging enough, but when we move to the national and global scene it is easy to get overwhelmed. Take the economy, for example. Every day it is in the news and it affects all of us, but "economic experts" disagree with each other about nearly everything. John Kenneth Galbraith, the long-time Harvard professor and iconic economist of the late twentieth century, reportedly said, "The only function of economic forecasting is to make astrology look respectable." [1]

Pessimists say that petroleum, which has powered the developed world for the past century, will run out in the twenty-first century, creating a potential energy crisis. Optimists say that our capacity to produce and use energy efficiently will increase in the decades ahead, creating new opportunity and wealth. Who's right? What will gas sell for next year, let alone in ten years?

Some economists predict we're on the edge of a fiscal meltdown with the stock market ready to crash and economic collapse right around the corner. Others project that the market will continue to rise, with greater prosperity in front of us. Some think unemployment and underemployment will make it tough to earn a living wage in the years ahead. Others think that the new economy will keep producing new jobs, with a bright future for tomorrow's workers. Who really knows?

What we do know is that we won't have any worries about the economy in heaven. No one will argue about fracking or get annoyed that gas prices just went up. We won't worry about disasters at power plants or disposing of nuclear waste. No one will follow the stock market or try to save money on groceries. No one will fret about getting enough hours at work or worry about losing their job. There will be no friction over income

---

1  *U.S. News & World Report,* March 7, 1988, 64. Other sources attribute this quote to the Stanford economist Ezra Solomon.

disparities between rich and poor. The pictures we're given of heaven tell us that there will always be enough for everyone there (Rev. 22:1–5).

## Terrorism and Corruption

Another set of global issues surrounds world politics. It seems there is always some sort of lethal conflict going on, especially in the Middle East. Recently, tens of thousands have died every year in Syria, Iraq, and Afghanistan. Everyone has their opinions on what started these conflicts and what might end them. For now they continue, surely to be followed by others.

Terrorism also remains a seemingly insoluble problem, with special attention given lately to the tens of thousands of civilians killed by ISIS, or the Islamic State. It's nice to know that in heaven there won't be any terrorists killing innocent civilians or military drones killing terrorists. No more "nights of terror" in Paris or anywhere else. In the midst of our fear and grief in this life, we can cling to the promise that in heaven there will be no more death, no more crying, and no more mourning of loved ones (Rev. 21:4). Again I'm struck with how heavenly heaven will be because of what is *not* there.

Even in places where terrorist activity is sparse, there are other political problems, such as government corruption. I learned this growing up in Louisiana. When I was in middle school and high school, our governor was Edwin Edwards. When accused of receiving illegal contributions, Edwards reportedly said, "it was illegal for them to give, but not for me to receive." Later, when it came to light that his wife had received $10 thousand in cash from a foreign businessman, Edwards maintained there was nothing wrong with friends giving each other gifts.

Despite his reputation for corruption, voters elected Edwards to third and fourth terms as governor. In his last election, Edwards ran against David Duke, a former Grand Wizard of the Knights of the Ku Klux Klan. The voters could choose between a man known for corruption and a man known as a neo-Nazi. A famous bumper sticker read, "Vote for the Crook. It's Important." I was glad my family had moved to Texas. The crook won in a landslide, served as governor, and was later found guilty of extortion, mail fraud, money laundering, racketeering, and wire fraud. He was incarcerated for approximately nine years, followed by two years on probation.

While Louisiana has some of the most spectacular cases in the U.S., they are a drop in the bucket when it comes to corruption worldwide. The World Bank estimates that more than $1 trillion in bribes are paid each year. This common practice flies in the face of God's instruction to "not accept a bribe, for a bribe blinds those who see and twists the words of the innocent" (Exod. 23:8; Deut. 16:19). Godly leaders should be more justice-motivated than money-motivated because "with the LORD our God there is no injustice or partiality or bribery" (2 Chron. 19:7).

In this world, corruption is commonplace. We hardly notice when yet another public official is indicted for misusing their position for unlawful private gain. And those are the ones who are caught. In this life injustice often goes unpunished, but not so on the Day of Judgment, when God will be praised for his judgments being true and just (Rev. 19:1–2). Moreover, in heaven no one will seek unlawful gain, but instead flourishing will be the "new normal." The absence of corruption and the presence of shalom in heaven are worth celebrating. There will be no more terrorism and no more corruption of any kind. Heaven is a place of complete justice and peace!

### The Race to End Racism

The U.S. now has black congressional representatives, black senators, and a black president—something that was practically unthinkable in the 1960s. A half-century ago only one in fifty marriages was interracial, whereas now it's closer to one in seven. Social patterns have changed and many African Americans have opportunities denied to them in the past. The same is true for Hispanic and Latino Americans, Asian Americans, Native Americans, and other racial and ethnic minorities in the U.S. Still, there's a long, long way to go.

Anger over police violence and racial tensions run high, whether it's in Ferguson, Baltimore, or elsewhere. The statistics on "institutional racism" are staggering. Starting in preschool and continuing through high school, black students are suspended at significantly higher rates than whites. Black juveniles are much more likely than whites to be sentenced as adults. Black men are searched more often at traffic stops than whites. Black college graduates are more likely to struggle to find jobs than white graduates. The median net worth of black and Latino households is less than a tenth (a tenth!) that of whites in the U.S. So, there's still a long, long way to go.

In the Bible, the book of James condemns discrimination between the rich and poor, which also has broader application to discrimination between people with other differences, such as our skin colors. James says, "Believers in our glorious Lord Jesus Christ must not show favoritism" (2:1) because that's an evil practice of discrimination (2:4). The contrast is clear for James: "If you really keep the royal law found in Scripture, 'Love your neighbor as yourself,' you are doing right. But if you show favoritism, you sin" (2:8–9). Love is right. Favoritism is wrong.

Racism treats some people as better than others, but the Bible teaches that all humans are made equally in God's image and likeness (Gen. 1:26–27; 5:1–3). The Bible also teaches that "the LORD does not look at the things people look at. People look at the outward appearance, but the LORD looks at the heart" (1 Sam. 16:7). God purposefully created people with differences, including beautiful variations among ethnicities, but all within one human race (Acts 17:26–28).

When racism rears its ugly head, people are divided and set

against each other, but in Christ people can be united. The Christian perspective is that "there is one body and one Spirit, just as you were called to one hope when you were called; one Lord, one faith, one baptism; one God and Father of all, who is over all and through all and in all" (Eph. 4:4–6). Jesus' followers of all skin colors have the same Father and are part of the same body. How much progress we'll make in overcoming racism on earth remains to be seen, but we know it won't exist at all in heaven.

Heaven will be inhabited by those from every tribe and language and people and nation, all of whom will surround the throne and worship God in unity together (Rev. 5:9; 7:9). All people groups are God's masterpieces, and in heaven the redeemed from all peoples will be united as God intended them to be from the beginning. In this life, racism makes us angry, bitter, weary, confused, and frustrated. I can't wait for heaven, where there won't be even a whiff of racism.

## Seeking to Stop Sexism

It's a similar story with sexism in the U.S. There has been progress in the past century, but there's still a long way to go. Women gained the right to vote in 1920, but they remain underrepresented (about 20%) in the House of Representatives and Senate. Most Americans now believe that women and men are equally suited to politics, but at the time of this writing we have not yet elected a female president or vice-president. Occupational opportunities are broader than they once were, but women still earn lower wages than their male counterparts. Married women are freer to work outside of the home, but working wives still do more of the housework than their husbands, creating a double burden or "second shift." It's no surprise, then, that working mothers get less sleep than working fathers.

Then there's the everyday sexism than we often consider "normal." Sexist humor may be frowned upon in some settings, but sexist jokes are still around. Too many women, walking or jogging along the sidewalk, still endure wolf whistling and street calling from men passing by in cars. Can't my daughters just go for a run without having to worry about perverts ogling them? In some workplaces women are still addressed as "darling" or "sweetheart." In many instances, women are encouraged to flirt, show a little cleavage, or giggle to get what they want. Ugh.

As bad as that is, it's nothing compared to the sex trade industry. Though it's officially illegal in most countries, millions of girls and women (and boys) are bought and sold into sex trafficking every year. Their stories, such as this one from a Cambodian teenager, are heart-rending:

> Tiger II ordered me to sell drugs from 9:00 P.M. to 11:00 P.M. and then sell my body from 11:00 P.M. to 4:00 A.M. I was ordered to steal, pickpocket, and cheat my customers by taking their money and motorbikes. They expected me to make $200 to $300 per night; if I did not, they punished me by stripping and beating me with a stick until I fainted, electrocuting me, cutting me and pouring salt water on the cuts, and placing my hands into a bamboo press for up to 20 minutes. . . . They forced me to sleep with as many as 50 customers a day. I had to give Tiger II all my money.[2]

Proverbs 31:8–9 tells us to "speak up for those who cannot speak for themselves, for the rights of all who are destitute; . . . defend the rights of the poor and needy." Thankfully there are many organizations and individuals who are speaking up for victims of sex trafficking and assisting survivors in rebuilding their lives. And thankfully, whether we are able to eliminate it completely in this life or not, we can be absolutely sure that there will be no more sex trafficking in heaven.

---

2 http://www.equalitynow.org/survivorstories/kolab_phalla. Retrieved 10/3/15.

No matter how we interpret "Babylon the Great" in the book of Revelation, we know that one of the despicable things God will overthrow at the end is "human beings sold as slaves" (Rev. 18:13). On the Day of Judgment, those who profited from buying and selling humans, alongside other "merchandise," will weep and mourn (Rev. 18:15), but the inhabitants of heaven will praise God for judging justly and righting every wrong (Rev. 19:1–4). There will be no more sexual immorality (Rev. 21:8; 22:15) and no more exploitation of vulnerable people in heaven. It's moving to imagine the endless joy, freedom, and love in heaven that is in such short supply for so many in this life.

## Environment on Earth and in Heaven

When we think about problems in the world today, many of us think of environmental issues. It took all of human history until around the year 1800 for the human population to reach one billion. By the 1920s we doubled to two billion. By the 1970s we doubled again to four billion. We are now closing in on another doubling at eight billion. In the beginning God told the first humans to "be fruitful and increase in number and fill the earth" (Gen. 1:28; 9:1). Some say that may be the one command of God that people have actually kept!

This growing population, alongside industrial pollution and inefficient agricultural practices, has led to a decrease in the overall water supply. Water stress is a daily reality for hundreds of millions in Africa and Asia. Even for regions where water is not scarce, access to usable water is an issue. While most of us can go three weeks without food, we'll die within a week without water. Water makes up more than half of our bodies and every living cell in our bodies requires water to function. It is a basic necessity to sustain and nourish human life.

In John's vision of the new heaven and the new earth, a prominent feature is abundant water. Jesus says, "to the thirsty I will give water without cost from the spring of the water of life" (Rev. 21:6; see also 22:17). It may not mean a lot to those of us who can just turn on the faucet and have drinkable water instantly, but to those living in a dry, barren land in the first century and to those who struggle in the twenty-first century day in and day out to access clean water, it's incredible news that all their thirsts, physical and spiritual, will be fully quenched in heaven! The beautiful picture of heaven includes "the river of the water of life, as clear as crystal, flowing from the throne of God and of the Lamb down the middle of the great street of the city" (Rev. 22:1–2). Whether we take it more literally or symbolically, the crystal-clear water of life, overflowing with sustenance and refreshment for God's people, will definitely make heaven heavenly.

Another set of environmental concerns in this life surrounds extreme weather events and adaptation to climate change. While debates are likely to continue about global warming and carbon management, everyone agrees that it's rough when a hurricane pummels the Philippines, a tornado rips through the U.S., a drought strikes Australia, or a flood overwhelms Pakistan. Tens of thousands are injured and die from these natural disasters every year. Of those who survive, the poor are usually hit the hardest because they live in vulnerable dwellings, are least likely to be covered by insurance, and have the fewest resources for rebuilding afterward.

As a kid, I was well-acquainted with hurricanes. We boarded up the windows and there was excitement in the air. I remember paddling around in our old kayak when pouring rains made the streets of New Orleans look like the canals of Venice. My mom was forced to evacuate for a month after Hurricane Katrina, and I have a vivid memory of clearing her yard and patching her roof. But we always recovered without major loss. Other people experience devastation and death when an earthquake rocks Haiti, a cyclone hits Myanmar, or a drought strikes East Africa. Many countries have no social safety net and people's roads back are incredibly long and hard.

All indications are that the original creation, from God's good hand, did not suffer the problems we experience now (Gen. 1–2). No earthquakes in Eden. The bad news is that when sin entered the world, the created order itself was affected (Gen. 3:17–19) in such a way that "the creation was subjected to frustration" (Rom. 8:20). The world as we know it today is not the way it was designed to be. Using a vivid metaphor, the apostle Paul says that "the whole creation has been groaning as in the pains of childbirth right up to the present time" (Rom. 8:22). Creation groans.

The good news is that "the creation itself will be liberated from its bondage to decay and brought into the freedom and glory of the children of God" (Rom. 8:21). Creation may be enslaved to corruption now, but the day of delivery from decay is coming. Together God's people and God's creation will be set free from the curse we live under! Jesus remains in heaven, we are told, "until the time comes for God to restore everything" (Acts 3:21), including the good creation.

There's a lot of speculation about what the weather will be like in heaven and whether there will be seasons there. The Bible doesn't say, but what we do know is that in the new heaven and the new earth (Rev. 21:1) God will make everything new (Rev. 21:5). It seems reasonable to assume that since there will be "no more death or mourning or crying or pain," the harmful extreme weather events we endure now will be part of the old order of things that will pass away (Rev. 21:4).

### Where Do We Find Our Hope?

Maybe you're like me and some days you don't feel up to watching the news or reading about it on the internet. A local company just closed up or laid people off, and they're going to have a tough time finding work. The economy is down and gas prices are up. More civilians have died at the hands of terrorists. Another politician has been indicted for corruption. Experts disagree sharply when they share their perspectives on the latest racial tension to flare up.

Or maybe during your commute home you kept mulling over yet another awkward sexist moment you've endured at work. When you sort through the mail you can't decide what to do with the solicitation to help dig new wells in Africa and the other envelope stamped with red alerts about the latest natural disaster and pressing needs in Asia. It can be depressing and overwhelming. After dinner if you watch the debates on TV or listen to the rants on talk radio you notice they seem to add more fuel to the fire rather than helping put the fires out.

When we're feeling engulfed by the crushing weight of the world's problems, where do we find hope? The Bible points God's people in the first century and the twenty-first century to "the hope stored up for you in heaven" (Col. 1:5). This is no "pie in the sky in the sweet by and by," no escapist hope that would cause us to neglect the pressing problems of this world. After all, the Paul who points us to the hope of heaven is the same Paul who spent years trudging through the ancient world to collect money for the poor in Jerusalem (Rom. 15:25–28; 2 Cor. 8–9).

In light of the coming victorious resurrection, we are encouraged right now to always give ourselves fully to the work of the Lord, because we know that our labor in the Lord is not in vain (1 Cor. 15:58). In the words of N. T. Wright, "Every prayer, all Spirit-led teaching, every deed that spreads the gospel, builds up the church, embraces and embodies holiness rather than corruption, and makes the name of Jesus honored in the world—all of this will find its way, through the resurrecting power of God, into the new creation that God will one day make."[3] The Holy Spirit gives God's people power to stare squarely at the world's problems, to work passionately for God's will to be done on earth as it is in heaven, and to overflow

---

3    N. T. Wright, *Surprised by Hope: Rethinking Heaven, the Resurrection, and the Mission of the Church* (New York: HarperCollins, 2008), 208.

with hope as we trust in the God of hope (Rom. 15:13). Not a single ounce of our labor in the Lord is in vain.

J. R. R. Tolkien's *The Return of the King* is a favorite of many readers and film critics. It narrates the dramatic defeat of the evil empire of the Dark Lord Sauron. In the fog and aftermath of the great battle, the doggedly persistent little hobbit Sam asks the mighty wizard Gandalf, "is everything sad going to come untrue?" Gandalf affirms that "a great Shadow has departed."[4] Even more importantly, the biblical answer to Sam's question is a resounding, hope-filled yes! In heaven all the world's problems will be resolved and everything sad will come untrue!

---

4   J. R. R. Tolkien, *The Return of the King* (New York: Ballantine, 1973), 246.

*For Individual Reflection or Group Discussion*

1. List a dozen social services needed in your community that will not be needed in heaven.

2. Which problems bother you the most as you consider the economy, terrorism, and political corruption? How does a heavenly perspective shape your approach to these problems?

3. How have you been touched, directly or indirectly, by racism, sexism, and ecological issues? What does the Bible teach about how these spheres of life will be transformed in heaven?

4. Name a few ways that we can bear witness to God's coming kingdom. When you consider the idea that "everything sad will come untrue," what comes into your mind and into your heart?

*What You Won't Find in Heaven*

## Interview with Michael Ayayo

**Brief Bio:** Michael is a licensed social worker who specializes in child welfare with the county services. He's married to Karelynne (next chapter) and is a valued Bible study leader at church.

*What is the hardest thing about your experience on earth in the people-helping profession?*

The hardest thing was helping to pack up the belongings of foster children whose foster mother had been rushed to the emergency room on Christmas Eve and died on Christmas Day. These were teenagers who thought they had finally found someone they could trust, who would be there for them. I remember not knowing how to comfort one of the boys, given our policy on physical contact, especially with children who have been abused. At the foster mother's funeral, he told me that this was a case when it would have been okay for me to have given him a hug.

*From your perspective as a people-helper, what do you most look forward to in heaven?*

I look forward to being out of a job. There will be no child welfare office in heaven because no one will be neglected or abused. No one will have bruises they are trying to hide. God "will wipe every tear from their eyes" (Rev. 21:4). Everyone will be family, because they will all call God their Father. No one will be homeless, because "my Father's house has many rooms" (John 14:2). I look forward to no more crises and no more need for on-call social workers in heaven.

*Share a time when, in your people-helping role, you had at least a "glimpse of heaven on earth."*

When children get to go home, it is a glimpse of heaven to me. I love reunifications where parents, with others' help, have so changed their behaviors and their homes that children will be safe. It's incredible when kids go back to a transformed home. I also love adoptions, when a child whose only "parent" was "the State" becomes a member of a new family. While it's hard, it's also exciting for these kids to be given a new name, a new identity, and a new future. I think of a 6-year-old who was at death's door—gray skin, yellowed eyeballs, and hundreds of small, sharp calcium deposits under her skin. The foster mother was there for the multiple-organ transplant surgery and then drove several hours daily to visit this little girl in the hospital during months of recovery. The last time I saw this girl her skin was pink, her eyes were white, and the bumps under her skin had been dissolved. There was still a long road of recovery, with some fear of organ rejection, but no fear of rejection from her foster mother, who was pursuing adoption.

### Interview with Sue Moroney

**Brief Bio:** Sue is a licensed school counselor who also volunteers as a guardian ad litem for foster children. She is the love of my life and is a respected counselor and Bible study leader at church.

*What is the hardest thing about your experience on earth in the people-helping profession?*

The hardest thing for me is seeing children suffer. Their suffering comes in so many forms, and much of it is due to the substance-abusing behaviors of the parents. To hear of kids living in filth, of enduring abuse by people they know and love, of experiencing their parents choosing a violent partner or a drug over regaining custody of them—these are heart-rending situations that are difficult for children to recover from. Sometimes I want to just shake the parents and say, "Do you realize how selfishly you are acting?" At the same time, I know from the background files that many of these parents had been children themselves in the system not too many years ago. The long-term family court judges and staff sometimes remember the sad cases about how these children-now-parents were raised. Generational sin, weakness, addiction, poverty, crime-ridden neighborhoods, and despair all become entangled into one painful, entrenched mess.

*From your perspective as a people-helper, what do you most look forward to in heaven?*

I look forward to heaven, where there will be no selfishness, no addiction, no crying or mourning or pain. I look forward to heaven, where no one will need to be afraid or lonely or hungry or cold. One day we won't need people trying to save children out of terrible situations, and we will be free to just soak in God's glory and radiance as we live in perfect peace with the Prince of peace.

*Share a time when, in your people-helping role, you had at least a "glimpse of heaven on earth."*

I see glimpses of heaven when I see children welcomed into loving foster homes and adopted into families that will love the children as their own. The unconditional love of strangers toward these children of varied races, disabilities and backgrounds, when they are sometimes not easy to love, is a glimpse of God's welcome to us as we join his family. The joy of belonging to someone who loves you and will care for you is one we can begin to experience now in human families and in God's family — the church. Later, in heaven, this joy of belonging will be complete and eternal!

# 6

## Who Is in Heaven and Why It Matters

AS WE'VE SEEN IN THE FIRST FIVE CHAPTERS, part of what makes heaven so heavenly is all the struggles that *won't* be there. But that's not the only word or the final word on heaven. Thinking about all the problems we'll leave behind will take us only so far in understanding heaven and getting excited about going there. Consider the analogy of a vacation. Sometime in the future, my wife and I hope to visit the state of Arizona. If we are able to go there during the month of March, a huge attraction is what *won't* be there, namely, weather in the 30s and gray slush that still remains from the last dregs of an Ohio winter. We'd look forward to leaving that behind.

But we also look forward to what we are hoping to experience in Arizona. A typical March day there is spent in sunshine in the 70s. Trip Advisor and other websites have whetted our appetites to drive the Red Rock Scenic Byway, explore the Grand Canyon, and swing by the Petrified Forest and Painted Desert. If this trip actually happens, we will probably spend the days leading up to it gathering more information about what it will be like, causing our anticipation to rise. It can work the same way with heaven. God's people are "saved *for* something as well as being saved *from* something."[1] We yearn for heaven not only because of all the problems that won't be there, but because of who is there, including God's angels, God's people, and God himself.

---

1   Jerry L. Walls, *Heaven: The Logic of Eternal Joy* (New York: Oxford University Press, 2002), 35. Italics in the original.

## Angels All Around

Angels are mentioned in half of the books of the Bible, with approximately three hundred references to angels scattered throughout Scripture. Their most common job is to carry God's messages to people. Another key function of holy angels is to accompany Jesus in his triumphant return from heaven to earth. Jesus told his followers, "The Son of Man is going to come in his Father's glory with his angels" (Matt. 16:27) and, "when the Son of Man comes in his glory, and all the angels with him, he will sit on his glorious throne" (Matt. 25:31). Paul also speaks of the time "when the Lord Jesus is revealed from heaven in blazing fire with his powerful angels" (2 Thess. 1:7). Angels appear with a much higher frequency in the book of Revelation (77 times) than in any other book of the Bible (the next highest is 24 times in the Gospel of Luke). In Revelation angels often reveal truth to John, carry out God's defeat of evil, and worship God.

There are lasting differences between angels and humans. The Son of God did not so love angels that he became an angel to redeem angels from their sin (Heb. 2:16–17). No angels were spared when they sinned, but rather they face judgment (2 Pet. 2:4; Jude 6). By contrast, the Son of God so loved people that he became a human to redeem his people from their sin (Gal. 4:4–5). Though commonly believed, the Bible never teaches that in heaven humans will become angels or that angels are the spirits of deceased loved ones looking down on us from heaven.

While there are lasting differences between angels and humans, one thing God's holy angels and God's holy people have in common is that they are both creatures who worship the same God (Ps. 103:19–22; Heb. 12:22–23). In John's vision of heaven "all the angels were standing around the throne and around the elders and the four living creatures. They fell down on their faces before the throne and worshiped God, saying: 'Amen! Praise and glory and wisdom and thanks and honor and power and strength be to our God for ever and ever. Amen!'" (Rev. 7:11–12).

I'm not much of a singer. In elementary school my music teacher wrote on my report card that "Steve sings with great enthusiasm within his ability." Translation: "He's loud and tone deaf." While I'm not quite as loud these days, I'm still off-key. Sometimes I apologize to the people in front of me at church before the singing ever gets started. It's a lot better if my voice can blend in with those behind me and around me. In heaven my voice will blend perfectly with the voices of all God's people and all God's holy angels (Rev. 5:8–14; 7:9–12). What a thrill that will be!

## Is That All We Will Do?

But will singing be our only activity in heaven? I've read a lot of books on heaven lately, and nearly every author raises the objection that an endless worship service sounds boring. A few suggest provocatively that one song after another would be closer to hell than to heaven. In an effort to paint a more attractive picture of the afterlife, some Christian authors have suggested that in the new heavens and the new earth we'll probably busy ourselves with the commercial exchange of goods and services that equitably distribute energy, clothing, and shelter,[2] or perhaps we'll enjoy purified versions of coffee, movies, and extreme sports.[3]

While possible, I consider these suggestions to be theological conjecture that drifts a bit from what is "expressly set down in Scripture, or by good and necessary consequence may be deduced from Scripture."[4] As Jon Laansma observes, "When it comes to heaven, the

---

2 Arthur O. Roberts, *Exploring Heaven: What Great Christian Thinkers Tell Us About Our Afterlife with God* (San Francisco: HarperCollins, 2003), 138–39.

3 Randy Alcorn, *Heaven* (Wheaton, IL: Tyndale, 2004), 297–98, 406–7, 410–13. As noted earlier, these speculations aside, I am a great admirer of how Randy Alcorn turns people's eyes toward heaven.

4 *The Westminster Confession of Faith*, Chapter I, section VI, as noted earlier in footnote 4 of the introduction.

line between sanctified imagination and idle speculation is thin."[5] What we know with certainty is that in heaven God will be present with his people (Rev. 21:3), and Scripture speaks of joy and eternal pleasures in God's presence (Pss. 16:11; 21:6), which seems incompatible with boredom. Boring worship in heaven? I don't think so. After all, we will be entering into our master's happiness (Matt. 25:21, 23). Commerce, coffee, and movies in heaven? I'm not so sure.

What we know for sure is that Jesus has made his people "to be a kingdom and priests to serve his God and Father" (Rev. 1:6). In the Old Testament we read of God's plan for Israel to "be for me a kingdom of priests" who are set apart to serve God (Exod. 19:6). In the New Testament we read of how Jesus' followers are "to be a holy priesthood, offering spiritual sacrifices acceptable to God through Jesus Christ" (1 Peter 2:5). So it's no surprise that heaven's inhabitants praise Jesus because he "purchased for God persons from every tribe and language and people and nation" and "made them to be a kingdom and priests to serve our God" (Rev. 5:9–10).

We are not told exactly what our priestly service to God in heaven will entail, but we can assume that those who "serve him day and night in his temple" (Rev. 7:15) will find it fulfilling. After all, Revelation 22:3 connects the fact that in heaven "no longer will there be any curse" with the fact that in heaven "his servants will serve him." Service sans sin will be satisfying. Whatever our service in heaven looks like, it will not bore us or be a grind, but will be a heavenly delight.

### God's Good Work in His People

When I think about the honor of serving Jesus in heaven, I feel woefully inadequate. I don't always do a very good job of serving

5   Jon Laansma, "Heaven in the General Epistles," in Christopher W. Morgan and Robert A. Peterson, eds., *Heaven* (Wheaton, IL: Crossway, 2014), 134.

him now. This is not to deny that by the Spirit's work I can see fruit in my life (Gal. 5:22–23) and experience a measure of victory over sin (Gal. 5:16). By God's grace, I am not the same person I was thirty years ago, ten years ago, or last year. I am grateful that, as Paul said, "it is God who works in you to will and to act in order to fulfill his good purpose" (Phil. 2:13). But I also identify with Paul's observation that "I do not do the good I want to do, but the evil I do not want to do—this I keep on doing" (Rom. 7:19). Too frequently, it's the same old me committing and confessing the same old sins over and over and over again.

I do things I shouldn't do and I fail to do things I should do. If there were charts for sins of commission and sins of omission, I think I would have run out of stickers for both of them. Then, even if I keep the rest of my behavior under control, I slip up with my tongue. I'm living proof that "no human being can tame the tongue" (James 3:8). I say things I shouldn't and I don't say things I should. Then, on the really good days when I keep the sinful actions and words to a minimum, I sin in my thoughts (Matt. 15:19). I might not be doing or saying things I shouldn't, but I'm definitely thinking things I shouldn't. Sinful pride, greed, anger, and lust much too often swirl through my mind, no matter how good I look on the outside. It's discouraging. My battle against sin has been going on longer than the Thirty Years War, and all too often I lose the battle.

I love how Paul says so confidently to the Philippian believers that "he who began a good work in you will carry it on to completion until the day of Christ Jesus" (Phil. 1:6). It reminds me that God is the one who saved me and is changing me. When I look at myself and see all the "good work" that remains to be done, it helps me to remember that God will finish what he started. Dan Schaeffer speaks for me, and perhaps for you too, when he makes the following observation:

> In many ways I am so far from our Lord's image in actual practice
> that I long for that part of heaven where I will be changed forever.

Earthly transformation is wearying work. I find that I am weary of my sin, weary of my failures, weary of my ignorance, weary of my shortcomings. . . . But one day you and I [as believers in Jesus] will be saved from the presence of sin itself. I will undergo a transformation of my being so cataclysmic that every microscopic vestige of sin will leave my entire being and never be able to find a home there again. I will not only be cleansed of all sin but forever become immune to it.[6]

In the midst of our ongoing battle with sin, all of God's people can cling tightly to God's promise that "as you eagerly wait for our Lord Jesus Christ to be revealed" you can be sure that "he will also keep you firm to the end, so that you will be blameless on the day of our Lord Jesus Christ" (1 Cor. 1:8–9). God is in the business of "bringing many sons and daughters to glory" because he is "the one who makes people holy" with the result that "Jesus is not ashamed to call them brothers and sisters" (Heb. 2:10–11). No more blame and no more shame, forever and ever!

And it gets even better. In some way, maybe through delegated authority, God's people will share in God's glorious reign. "If we endure, we will also reign with him" (2 Tim. 2:12). Jesus promises his followers that "to the one who is victorious, I will give the right to sit with me on my throne, just as I was victorious and sat down with my Father on his throne" (Rev. 3:21). Sitting with Jesus on his throne!

When Jesus has made his followers to be a kingdom and priests, we are told "they will reign on the earth" (Rev. 5:10). Perhaps Jesus was hinting at this when he said, "blessed are the meek, for they will inherit the earth" (Matt. 5:5). The final chapter of the Bible describes Jesus' servants in heaven by saying, "they will reign for ever and ever" (Rev. 22:5). Again, there is a lot of speculation about what it will look like for us to reign in heaven, but we know it will be thrilling!

---

6  Dan Schaeffer, *A Better Country: Preparing for Heaven* (Grand Rapids: Discovery House, 2008), 119, 122.

## Keeping It Together

According to Jesus, the first and greatest commandment is to love God with our whole selves and the second is like it, to love our neighbor as ourselves (Matt. 22:37–39). In Jesus' words, "all the Law and the Prophets hang on these two commandments" (Matt. 22:40). Love of God and neighbor should be kept together here on earth, and they should also be kept together in the new heavens and the new earth. But in our understanding of heaven, it's possible for us to put so much emphasis on loving God that we neglect loving people, or vice versa.[7]

Especially in the past, many theologians put the emphasis in heaven on "the beatific vision," a direct vision of the divine essence or seeing God face to face. This left many with the impression that our only activity in heaven will be contemplating God in his heavenly glory, with people and other things being unimportant. More recently, many authors have put the emphasis in heaven on our activities and relationships with other people. They sometimes portray heaven as enjoying an improved version of our favorite earthly activities, with God receding into the background. We can mistakenly begin to love our hopes for heaven more than the God who lovingly rules heaven.

Kenneth Boa and Robert Bowman put it nicely when they say, "The extremes of a purely God-centered view of heaven as endless contemplation of the Divine and a purely man-centered view of heaven as an unending theme park adventure with our earthly family and friends must both be rejected."[8] Heaven would not be heaven without people and heaven would not be heaven without God. *The Book of Common Prayer* hits the right note when it describes how, in heaven, God's people will experience "the joy of fully knowing and

---

7 Colleen McDannell and Bernhard Lang, *Heaven: A History*, 2nd ed. (New Haven, CT: Yale University Press, 2001), especially 353–58.

8 Kenneth D. Boa and Robert M. Bowman Jr., *Sense and Nonsense about Heaven and Hell* (Grand Rapids: Zondervan, 2007), 168–69.

loving God and each other."[9] So we will make it our aim to keep these two glorious realities together in the following sections as we consider how God's people will love each other and how we will love God forever in heaven.

## God's Perfected People

By God's grace, I am already a new creation in Christ (2 Cor. 5:17), but sin is still so "second nature" to me that I can hardly imagine what it will be like when God has finished his good work in me. Instead of wanting the wrong thing (people's praise), I'll want the right thing (God's glory). Instead of doing the wrong thing (lazily indulging myself), I'll do the right thing (loving someone else). Instead of saying the wrong thing (stretching the facts), I'll say the right thing (speaking plain truth). Instead of thinking the wrong thing (why I'm better than them), I'll think the right thing (appreciating God's gifts in them).

Imagine: Everything I desire, everything I do, everything I say, and everything I think only being right, good, and holy. Not just once in a while but all the time. The mind-blowing truth is that when God has fully glorified me, I'll actually be like Jesus (Rom. 8:29–30). Not just for a minute or an hour—but forever and ever.

In heaven, by God's grace, I and all of God's people will fully bear the image of Jesus Christ, the heavenly man (1 Cor. 15:49). That means that our relationships in heaven will look radically different than they do in this life. Sure, we get glimpses of true love now, "because God's love has been poured out into our hearts through the Holy Spirit" (Rom. 5:5). But our motivations are typically tainted by selfishness, and our relationships now are stained by sin. In heaven, every single person we come into contact with will image Jesus in glorious ways. There will be no more dodging that person who rubs

---

9   *The Book of Common Prayer* (New York: Oxford University Press, 1979), 862.

you the wrong way. And no more being that annoying person whom other people politely "choose not to spend time with."

Jesus gives us a beautiful picture of how "many will come from the east and the west, and will take their places at the feast with Abraham, Isaac and Jacob in the kingdom of heaven" (Matt. 8:11). God's people from all over the globe will join together in this magnificent feast in the kingdom of heaven. We will enjoy harmonious relationships marked by righteousness, peace, and joy in the Holy Spirit (Rom. 14:17). We will really love our heavenly neighbors as ourselves. Not just some of them, some of the time. All of them. All of the time. It will be heaven!

Our love for God will also be purified in heaven. In this life we often love God with half our hearts, or maybe in a really good moment, with most of our hearts. In heaven, perhaps for the first time ever, we will truly love God with all of our heart, mind, soul, and strength (Mark 12:30). Not 50% or even 90%, but 100%. We'll actually keep the first and greatest commandment (Matt. 22:37–38), and we won't need a preacher or a book to remind us to do it. Loving God and loving people will come naturally when love has been made complete among us and we have been made perfect in love (1 John 4:17–18).

## God at the Center

Last summer I had the chance to help lead college students on a service-learning trip to France. We started out with a few days in Paris. While the Louvre museum is near to the geographic center, and the Arc de Triomphe is a sort of symbolic center, many consider the Eiffel tower the central gathering place in Paris. The night we went, thousands of people from dozens of countries encircled the tower, with everyone's face turned toward it, gazing upward in amazement as the lights sparkled in the night. The tower drew us together, if only for a while.

From Paris we traveled to a famous monastery in Taizé, France. The center of this community is the church sanctuary, where everyone gathers for communal prayers morning, noon, and night. We scattered for our different jobs, meetings, and meals, but what brought the whole community together was a shared time of prayer at the beginning, middle, and end of each day. As "pilgrims" who had gathered from nearly every continent, we chanted common prayers in at least a half-dozen languages (with translations available, to understand the meaning). But this experience of community was also temporary, as we departed for home at the end of the week.

I enjoy more lasting community in my local church with the worshipers at Parkside Church Green Campus. In fact, I am working on this chapter from our sanctuary on a Sunday morning as a reminder of why we assemble for worship and what we have in common. It's 8:30 A.M., two hours before the service begins, but a dozen people are checking the static on the bass and coordinating their vocals so that they can lead us through worship in song. Our lead pastor has also been here for several hours, going over his sermon and praying for God's manifest presence among us. Hundreds of others are preparing themselves at home for our worship gathering.

Gathering with God's people on earth gives us a taste of what it will be like to gather with God's people in heaven, where the center of it all will be God himself. We will no longer be plagued by self-centeredness as we are now. Instead we will all be centered on God. Besides the company of God's holy angels and God's holy people, the central attraction of heaven is God himself.

In the Old Testament, the Psalmist cries out, "Whom have I in heaven but you? And earth has nothing I desire besides you" (73:25). Psalm 27:4 declares, "One thing I ask from the LORD, this only do I seek: that I may dwell in the house of the LORD all the days of my life, to gaze on the beauty of the LORD and to seek him in his temple." In the New Testament, the apostle Paul likewise says he "would prefer to be away from the [earthly] body and at home with the Lord" (2 Cor. 5:8). The reason he says "I desire to depart" for heaven is because he will then "be with Christ, which is better by far" (Phil. 1:23).

This deep longing of God's people from every era will be realized in heaven, when we are at home with the Lord. A perfect home to be enjoyed by all of God's family. There are currently fifty million refugees worldwide, but God's people who have been homeless or forced to wander as refugees will suffer no more displacement or sleepless nights exposed to harsh elements. God's people who were unwanted or disowned by their earthly parents ("wards of the state") will have a place of belonging and love in their heavenly home. It's moving to consider that in heaven we won't just be in the same place as Jesus but will actually be with Jesus. He comforts his followers by telling us, "I will come back and take you to be with me" (John 14:3). To be with Jesus Christ is better by far!

## King of Kings

Everybody has their favorite world leader. In the past hundred years, Nelson Mandela, Martin Luther King Jr., and Mahatma Gandhi were especially revered. Some wish nostalgically that Franklin Roosevelt, Abraham Lincoln, or George Washington was still president. Despite these leaders' flaws, many people grieved when their lives came to an end.

It won't be like that in heaven, when our flawless, perfect King will never be assassinated or voted out of office. Every creature in heaven says: "To him who sits on the throne and to the Lamb be praise and honor and glory and power, for ever and ever!" (Rev. 5:13). Heavenly worship declares, "praise and glory and wisdom and thanks and honor and power and strength be to our God for ever and ever" (Rev. 7:12). God's glorious reign will never come to an end!

On the flip side, not only have revered leaders been lost, but wicked leaders have perpetrated evil. In this life, much too often "the kings of the earth rise up and the rulers band together against the LORD and against his anointed" (Ps. 2:2). We think of the twentieth-century horrors wrought upon millions of innocents by Joseph Stalin, Adolf Hitler, and Mao Zedong. Such reigns of terror will all be reversed forever when "the kingdom of the world has become the kingdom of our Lord and of his Messiah, and he will reign for ever and ever" (Rev. 11:15). A perfect king ruling over a perfect kingdom forever and ever! I want to see that for myself.

### The Invisible Becomes Visible

God is invisible to us now (1 Tim. 1:17) because God is the one "who lives in unapproachable light, whom no one has seen or can see" (1 Tim. 6:16). Most theologians believe that we are restricted from seeing God now because in our sinful state we could not see perfectly holy God and live (Exod. 33:20). But that will change in heaven when God has purified us from all sin. Job declares that "after my skin has been destroyed, yet in my flesh I will see God; I myself will see him with my own eyes" (19:26–27). John says similarly that "when Christ appears, we shall be like him, for we shall see him as he is" (1 John 3:2). To be like Jesus and see him as he is!

As John reports his vision of heaven, "The throne of God and of the Lamb will be in the city, and his servants will serve him. They will see his face" (Rev. 22:3–4). While it is not the only thing we will do in heaven, seeing God's face is perhaps the greatest blessing of all. Seeing God's face represents an incredibly close communion with the Lord, long hoped for (Ps. 11:7). Consider

> How glorious it will be to look upon the face of Him who loved us and gave Himself for us, who has lived to make intercession for us, the One who fought many battles and won them all, in whose life there has never been one single moment of sin of any kind, in

word or deed or thought, whose face will be radiant with unbroken victory, with unquenchable love and with perfect obedience to the holy will of God.[10]

The potentially closest relationship on earth, the healthy love and intimacy between a husband and wife, gives us an inkling of how close our relationship with the Lord will be (Eph. 5:25–32). Jesus' followers are said to be his bride, the ones upon whom he has set his eternal love, with heaven as the great wedding between Jesus and his people (Rev. 19:7–9; 21:2, 9). It's hard to imagine being that close to Jesus, and not just for a moment, but forever and ever and ever.

Heaven is appealing because sin and all of its horrible effects will be eliminated. But heaven is also attractive because God's holy angels, God's holy people, and God himself will be there. In John's climactic description of heaven, we are told that "God's dwelling place is now among the people, and he will dwell with them. They will be his people, and God himself will be with them and be their God" (Rev. 21:3). God will dwell with us forever!

We will serve God with glad, willing spirits in ways that fill our hearts with joy. God will finish his work of perfecting his people so that we truly love others and love God with our whole selves. A magnificent thing about heaven is getting to be with Jesus Christ, which is far better than anything we've experienced in this life. On top of all that, we will enjoy the splendor of seeing God's face and basking in his loving presence forever. Come quickly, Lord Jesus!

---

10 Wilbur M. Smith, *The Biblical Doctrine of Heaven* (Chicago: Moody Press, 1968), 254.

## For Individual Reflection or Group Discussion

1. What are some speculative ideas about heaven that you've had or that you've heard from others that go beyond what we read in Scripture or what we can deduce from Scripture?

2. Dan Schaeffer says, "I will undergo a transformation of my being so cataclysmic that every microscopic vestige of sin will leave my entire being and never be able to find a home there again." What are some changes in yourself you would love to experience in heaven?

3. When you think about heaven, what naturally comes to your mind: God or other people? Explain your understanding of how we will serve God and fellowship with people in heaven.

4. What do you think it will be like for all of God's perfected people to gather around his throne in heaven? In what way do you look forward to seeing God's face and being with him forever?

6. *Who Is in Heaven and Why It Matters*

## Interview with Jonathan Holmes

**Brief Bio:** Pastor Jonathan Holmes possesses a rare blend of intellectual breadth, spiritual depth, and relational warmth. I am honored to call him my pastor and my friend.

*In your experience teaching the Bible, what are people's common misunderstandings of heaven?*

That heaven is a faraway place disconnected from anything in this created world; that in heaven we will be spiritual beings floating around in some ethereal setting; that in heaven we will experience an intensified version of our favorite earthly hobbies, without any real focus on Jesus Christ; that heaven is about individuals in our own mansions, not the corporate people of God.

*From your perspective as a pastor and teacher, what do you most look forward to in heaven?*

I can't wait to see what it looks like to worship God wholly (with our full physical, emotional, mental, and spiritual capacities) and to love purely with desires that are rightly ordered. I'm also curious to see what the new creation looks like. I'm excited to experience what it will be like to always excel and grow in our love for God and others. As a counselor, I look forward to people no longer suffering, with the former things not even being remembered (Isa. 65:17).

*Share a time, in your pastor-teacher role, when you had at least a "glimpse of heaven on earth."*

My first time in Bolivia at a Spanish worship service gave me a glimpse of people from every tribe, tongue, and nation worshiping God. While our cultural expressions vary, we share a common object of worship—God! Another "glimpse of heaven on earth" was seeing the birth of my four daughters and the joy it brings. That was a taste of the joys we will experience in heaven—joys that are pure, holy, good, right, and unadulterated. As C. S. Lewis said, "Joy is the serious business of heaven."

## Interview with Karelynne Ayayo

**Brief Bio:** Dr. Karelynne Ayayo is associate professor of New Testament at Palm Beach Atlantic University. Our church is blessed by her gentle spirit and her skilled teaching of God's word.

*In your experience teaching the Bible, what are people's common misunderstandings of heaven?*

That we came from heaven (pre-existing in some way) and are going "back" there; that in heaven we will change from being humans to being angels; that in heaven we will still be married to our spouses and parents of our children in the same way that we are here in this life; that heaven is located physically up in the sky; that we should take all the biblical imagery of heaven literally (streets of gold, etc.); that heaven is more about what I'll get and what I'll experience than it is about God.

*From your perspective as a Bible professor, what do you most look forward to in heaven?*

I look forward to being in the presence of the full revelation of God, no longer facing all the limitations of relating to God that we do now. We will no longer need to doubt our interpretations of Scripture or our spiritual experiences, which we do now as we work with only a partial revelation of God. I also look forward to being done with the battle of sin, fatigue, and the struggles of life in this fallen world. No more daily challenges with myself or with others.

*Share a time when, in your role as a professor, you had at least a "glimpse of heaven on earth."*

I had the privilege of teaching a student in four different courses even though he did not major in Bible. We had many debates over the years but eventually he came to Christ in my office. I'll never forget the radiant peace on his face, a sign of his beginning life in God's kingdom, with a foretaste of things to come. What a moment to see God's power draw him from darkness to light!

# Appendix 1

## Recent Visits to Heaven and Back?

LATELY, CONTROVERSIAL IDEAS ABOUT HEAVEN have been going around. A lot of the ideas have been spawned by books that report the details of people's supposed visits to heaven. At the time I wrote this appendix, these books were available at our local LifeWay Christian Resources store in Canton, Ohio, where I worked from an overstuffed chair. There I was surrounded by thousands of books, but the ones I've been reading recently are the bestsellers that describe how people visited heaven and returned to tell about it. This appendix summarizes four gripping stories and then shows some problems with relying on them for what we believe about heaven.

### A Minister Tells about His Trip to Heaven

Evangelist Jesse Duplantis wrote a book called *Heaven: Close Encounters of the God Kind,* in which he gives the details from his "trip to heaven" one afternoon in August 1988. As Jesse tells it, he was zoomed from his hotel room to heaven by a horseless chariot. Jesse says that heaven had snow that was not cold, flowers that could not be crushed, and copper-colored fruit that was needed to sustain weakened people who had believed in Jesus but had not lived life as they should have to its fullest potential. Those people still had lessons to learn in heaven, after which they would be able to go to God's throne. Jesse relates how he himself repeatedly had to partake of this juicy, copper-colored fruit in order to be strengthened and withstand God's glory.

While in heaven, Jesse says he met many people one might expect to meet there. Abraham was there to give Jesse a drink. Jonah taught Jesse that disobedience on earth causes us delays in reaching the level God has planned for us in heaven. David was the only one besides Jesus to wear a crown, and David was assigned to take Jesse around heaven and serve him. David had an infectious smile and a hardy laugh. Jesse and David talked about their common interest in music. David admitted some regret at having complained a bit too much in singing about his troubles, rather than singing more about God's answers to his problems. Jesse was surprised to see how short Paul was, his feet not even reaching the ground from the bench where he sat.

Jesse says Jesus was taller than Paul, somewhere between 5'11" and 6'1," with light brown hair and holes in his feet about the size of a nickel. Jesus preached a message to those in heaven, but rather than the quiet, mild-mannered, calm delivery that Jesse expected, Jesus preached with great emotion and dynamism. As Jesus shouted and hollered excitedly about going to earth to bring more people back to heaven, the people in heaven screamed and howled in response. Afterward Jesse had the chance to compliment Jesus on his great message. Jesus explained that the purpose of Jesse's trip to heaven was for him to understand how important it was for him to go back to earth to tell people that Jesus is coming again. Jesse came to realize how much God needed him to reach other people. In fact, Jesus even told him straight out, "I need you, Jesse."

Jesse also reports seeing the heavenly Book of Life, which was about 5½ feet high, a supersized book compared with anything on display here at LifeWay. Jesse says he was allowed to see his own personal home in heaven, with manicured grass, a water fountain in the yard, a stunning foyer, and great furniture. Jesse learned that families live together in heaven and they occasionally go on picnics. Jesse says he even saw God the Father sitting on the throne. While he did not see God's face, Jesse says he saw the lower part of God's hand, which was huge. In fact, Jesse says that when God's finger barely moved, an angel that happened to be flying nearby was tossed against a wall, with a crashing sound of bam. Thankfully the angel was not hurt.

While Jesse reported no lasting physical harm in heaven, he noted that there still could be some hard things experienced there. Having seen God the Father and God the Son, Jesse recalls asking a dumb question about where the Holy Spirit was. When an angel answered that the Holy Spirit was on the earth, Jesse says he felt really stupid and he still feels embarrassed about it. Later, Jesus expressed how he dreaded judgment day, which would be the worst day of his life because he would have to tell part of the creation he loved to depart from him. As Jesus' eyes welled up with tears, Jesse could tell Jesus was hurting. So Jesse put his hand on Jesus to comfort him.

Then it was time to head back to earth on the chariot, but Jesus told David to take Jesse back by way of the heavenly mountains. There Jesse found out that many people have an apartment or condo in the heavenly countryside, besides their mansion in the Holy City. Every desire is met. It must have been a shock for Jesse to find himself back in a standard room in the Best Western Motel in Magnolia, Arkansas! With a glance at the clock radio, Jesse realized that the whole trip to heaven had taken just a little over five hours. Of course, Jesse knew immediately that there would be skeptics when he went public with his experience. Nonetheless, he insists that "it literally happened" and that others have since confirmed that "they have been to heaven and have seen the very places I described."[1] Jesse, now in his sixties, remains active as "the apostle of joy," an evangelist and revivalist who reaches millions with his weekly video broadcasts.

---

1   Jesse Duplantis, *Heaven: Close Encounters of the God Kind* (Tulsa, OK: Harrison House, 1996), 147, 151.

## *Another Minister Tells about a Shorter Trip to Heaven*

Less than half a year after Jesse's experience, in January 1989 Pastor Don Piper reported a similar experience of going to heaven for a while and then coming back to earth to tell about it. While Jesse's heavenly trip lasted more than five hours, Don's was just an hour-and-a-half, as detailed in his *New York Times* bestseller, *90 Minutes in Heaven.* As Don, then 38 years old, drove back from an annual state-wide church conference, through no fault of his own he was killed instantly when an eighteen-wheel truck crossed the center line on a two-lane bridge and crushed his car. Those who examined Don, including trained paramedics, found no pulse and declared him dead.

Don does not recall the accident. After driving along the bridge, his next reported memory is being enveloped by a brilliant light and standing in heaven. What Don says he saw there is quite different from what Jesse says he saw. Don did not see any snow that's not cold, uncrushable flowers, or copper-colored fruit. Rather, in front of a decorative gate, Don saw a big crowd of smiling people praising God and rushing toward Don, a sort of heavenly welcoming party.

Unlike Jesse's encounters with biblical characters, everyone Don met were people he had known during his life on earth but who had died before he did. Don's heavenly greeters were all people who had exercised a positive spiritual influence on him—helping him to become a Christian or encouraging him to grow as a Christian. Interestingly, each person Don saw in heaven was the precise age they had been when Don last saw them on earth, though their physical features were now perfected and lovely to look at. There was a wide variety of ages there. His grandfather had a head full of white hair, sparkling eyes, and a grin from ear to ear as he hugged Don.

Everyone there radiated unimaginable serenity, vitality, and joy, including Don's great-grandmother. In her later years she had been humped over by her osteoporosis, with a wrinkled face and false teeth. Now in heaven she stood perfectly upright, the wrinkles were smoothed out, and her teeth shone brightly (somehow Don knew they were not false teeth). At times, Don was speechless as he absorbed the loving welcome and took it all in. It was like the family gatherings Don had experienced on earth but amped up several notches, a sort of reunion on steroids, but entirely positive, without the mixture of good and bad we have on earth. Even though there was no city mansion or country condo (as with Jesse), Don felt he was at home, where he belonged.

Gradually the welcoming crowd and Don moved together toward the brilliant, intense light that came out from the heavenly gate in front of them. As they moved, Don was engulfed by music that permeated his body, as though it was playing in him and through him. Amazingly, there were hundreds of songs simultaneously being sung in worship of God. Don was not sure whether the source was angelic or human, but he heard words such as "praise," "glory to God," and "hallelujah" sprinkled through the songs. Don estimates there may have been thousands of heavenly songs, each of which was distinct but also perfectly harmonious when sung together. When Don has flashbacks of his heavenly experience, it is the sounds that stand out more than the sights or even the hugs from loved ones. And when Don finds himself longing to return to heaven, he says, above everything else he longs to hear again those incredible unending songs.

Unlike Jesse, Don did not see God or a glowing light that would indicate God's concentrated presence. Looking back on his experience, Don believes that once people have actually seen God or been in God's direct presence, they will not ever return to earth and its comparative emptiness. Though others in heaven spoke of going in and out of the gate, Don only peeked through it with a yearning to see more. Just as Don was about to pass through the gates into heaven itself, he found himself back on earth, critically injured but alive, in response to the prayers of another pastor, despite the EMTs' pronouncement an hour and a half earlier that Don was dead.

As Don came to earthly consciousness again, he found himself singing the hymn "What a Friend We Have in Jesus" with the faith-filled pastor who had prayed for him. The EMTs confirmed that Don was alive and he was rushed by ambulance to a hospital. There he underwent nearly three dozen surgeries in the midst of an excruciatingly painful recovery. As Don summarizes it, "I had experienced heaven, returned to earth, and then suffered through the closest thing to hell on earth I ever want to face."[2] Not until a few years later, at the prompting of a trusted friend, did Don cautiously begin to share the story of his ninety minutes in heaven. Still ministering in his sixties, Don has been pleased to be able to reassure believers that heaven is real and to prompt skeptics seriously to consider the afterlife. His books have sold more than six million copies in dozens of languages, and a movie adaptation of his story was released in the fall of 2015.

## A Young Boy Also Tells about His Visit to Heaven

Outstripping Don's bestseller is Todd Burpo's recent *Heaven Is for Real*, topping ten million copies sold in forty languages, making it the most popular book of the past decade printed by an evangelical Christian publisher. Hollywood turned the book into a movie that made $90 million, headlined by actor Greg Kinnear, who plays Todd Burpo. The story is that in March 2003 Todd's 3-year-old son Colton Burpo suffered a ruptured appendix. Four months after his appendectomy Colton began to tell his parents about how, during his surgery, he went to heaven. Unlike Don's case, none of the medical personnel ever indicated that Colton died before his trip to heaven.

In various conversations with his parents, scattered over the next couple of years, Colton provided many details of his time in heaven. These details came out slowly, in response to his parents' attempts at

2   Don Piper, *90 Minutes in Heaven: A True Story of Death and Life* (Grand Rapids: Revell, 2004), 62.

open-ended, non-suggestive questions. Unlike his older predecessors Jesse (a little more than five hours) and Don (one and a half hours), Colton says that he was in heaven for just three minutes. But, as he reports it, quite a lot happened during those 180 seconds.

Colton said one of the angels looked like his Grandpa Dennis but without the glasses. As Colton tells it, nobody wears glasses in heaven and nobody is old there, in contrast with Don's report of his white-haired grandfather. Colton's dad Todd, the author of the book, considers it good news that we will be a younger version of ourselves in heaven, with only a few exceptions, such as Colton's stillborn sister, who will be an older version of their in-utero selves in heaven. Colton reports that there are lots of kids in heaven. He says that all the people and angels there have wings they use to fly, except for Jesus, who is wingless and moves up and down like an elevator.

Whereas Jesse saw mainly Bible figures in heaven (Abraham, Jonah, David, etc.) and Don saw mainly people who had been positive spiritual influences on him (a grandfather, classmate, and teachers), Colton reported a mixture of the two groups. He met John the Baptist, who was nice. He also saw Mary, Jesus' mother, who was sometimes kneeling before God's throne and at other times standing next to Jesus, whom she still loved like a mom. Colton met his great-grandfather, Pop, who had died before Colton was born. Colton's parents were surprised that Pop had been able to recognize his great-grandson, since Colton was not born until decades after Pop had died.

Colton's parents were also astonished when he told them he had two sisters, since they had never spoken to him about the child his mother had miscarried. Colton says he met his baby sister in heaven. She showered Colton with hugs and said she couldn't wait for her parents to come there. Having met his stillborn sister, Colton at times missed her to the point of tears once he was back on earth.

Colton says that part of his time in heaven was spent sitting in Jesus' lap. According to Colton, Jesus had brown hair, a full but casual beard, and greenish-blue eyes. Colton told his parents how Jesus wore a crown of gold with a pink diamond in the middle, and how he was the only one in heaven sporting a purple sash. Jesus' clothes were white and Colton said Jesus had red "markers" on the palm of each hand and the top of each foot. Jesus was Colton's teacher in heaven, and doing the homework that Jesus assigned was Colton's favorite activity in heaven.

God's throne was huge, Colton said, because God was the biggest one in heaven. Jesus sits in a chair to the right of his Dad's throne and the angel Gabriel sits on the left side of God's throne. Gabriel is really nice. Colton himself sat in a special little chair next to God the Holy Spirit—who Colton says is definitely there in heaven, not just on the earth as Jesse was told earlier. Colton had difficulty describing the Holy Spirit, other than saying "he's kind of blue."[3]

Colton said that he saw Satan outside of heaven, but he refused to describe what Satan looked like. Besides reflecting back on his time in heaven, Colton also claims to have seen the future war in which Jesus, good angels, and good men will defeat Satan, the monsters, and bad people. Colton explained that the women and children would be bystanders in this heavenly war, but Colton's father would participate in this fight, using either a sword or a bow and arrows.

Like Jesse and Don, Colton's family was reluctant to go public with their story. In fact, they waited nearly four years after Colton's three-minute experience to speak about it to groups outside of the family. Since then the Burpos' Heaven is For Real ministry has hit the big time. They not only have the best-selling book by an evangelical Christian publisher in the past decade and a Hollywood movie to tell their story. In addition, Colton, now a teenager, joins his parents in singing and speaking at events in the U.S. and worldwide. Their influence is considerable.

---

3 Todd Burpo, *Heaven Is for Real: A Little Boy's Astounding Story of His Trip to Heaven and Back* (Nashville: Thomas Nelson, 2010), 103.

## *Another Young Boy Tells about His Multiple Visits to Heaven*

Just as Jesse's experience in 1988 was followed by Don's in 1989, so Colton's experience in 2003 was followed by that of Alex Malarkey in 2004. Alex's dad failed to see oncoming traffic at a dangerous intersection, leading to a terrible accident. Alex, then 6 years old, had severe spinal column damage and was in a coma for two months. After coming out of it and slowly regaining the ability to communicate, Alex told his parents about his time in heaven, which began as an out-of-body experience at the time of the accident but was followed by other visits to heaven — all reported in the *New York Times* bestseller *The Boy Who Came Back from Heaven*.

Interestingly, Alex's dad Kevin had told his little son about Don Piper's earlier experience. After his accident, Alex echoed the glorious music and stunning colors in heaven, but he did not see many humans whom he had known on earth. Unlike Don, Alex says he saw only angels, Jesus, God, and people from the Bible (without further elaboration), a difference which Alex attributes to Don staying outside of heaven's gates whereas Alex reports arriving inside of heaven's gates. The outer heaven is a sort of waiting room that has within it a hole that goes to hell, while the inner heaven that Alex saw is more bright, intense, and colorful than the area that Don visited. Also, Alex says he did not experience heavenly music as multiple, simultaneous, harmonious songs, as Don did, but rather as extremely intense, marked by especially beautiful harps.

During his post-accident operation, Alex says, Jesus took him to heaven where one hundred fifty pure, white angels called his name. There in heaven Alex says he saw God the Father up to the neck, but that seeing God's face will only come later. Alex reports that God has a large, human-like body that is covered in a bright white robe. According to Alex, God never leaves his throne in the heavenly temple. Unlike Colton's story in which the angel Gabriel is next to God's throne, in Alex's story the angel Michael is in that spot. Eventually, Alex says, Jesus accompanied him back to the hospital, where he held Alex in the emergency room and kept him from being afraid.

Besides his time in heaven, Alex reports extensive interaction with angels on earth as well. According to Alex, some angels are warriors, others worshipers, others messengers, and the toughest ones are guardians of heaven's walls. The angels who visited Alex during his recovery performed different jobs, for example, helping him breathe, helping him form words, holding his head steady, and singing with him. Angels are winged, white, and vary in size from two feet on up, according to Alex. Alex reports that the angels chat not only about him but about themselves as well, so that he has come to know several of them by name: John, Ryan, Vent, etc.

Alex also says that during the car accident he encountered the devil. Unlike Colton, who refused to tell others what the devil looked like, Alex provided a detailed description. According to Alex, the devil is three-headed, with each head topped with hair of fire and each head spewing out different lies simultaneously. He has red eyes, a nasty torn-up nose, and a few moldy teeth in a funny-looking mouth. His bony limbs are covered by torn and dirty robes. Alex says demons resemble the devil, but they are often green and have long fingernails. There is constant spiritual warfare, which is sometimes so busy that it prevents Alex from being able to visit heaven.

In a major contrast from the one-time visits of Jesse, Don, and Colton, Alex and his father report that he has gone to heaven several times. Typically he arrives just inside the gates where he chats with the angels, who usually speak excitedly about the day Jesus will come back to the earth. Then Alex enters the heavenly temple where he speaks with God himself. Sometimes angels are present but other times Alex converses privately with God, until the Lord lets him know that the visit is done. These visits to heaven usually occur when Alex is sleeping.

While Alex is free to pass on much of what he saw in heaven, he claims to have been prohibited from communicating other details. He sees himself as a blend of the apostle John, who conveyed aspects of what he saw in heaven, and Paul who was not permitted to share other things. Alex states that "heaven is not the next world; it is now. Heaven is not up in the sky; it is everywhere and nowhere. Heaven is a place that is not a place."[4] But when asked whether heaven is a physical place, Alex also responds, "How could I have been there if it wasn't?"[5]

According to Alex's dad, his son's account is cohesive and always consistent. Others have a different view. His parents' marriage is broken, and Alex's mother has repeatedly said that the words in the book are not Alex's words, but rather an embellished and twisted version of his account. In January of 2015 Alex wrote an open letter in which he stated, *"I did not die. I did not go to heaven. I said I went to heaven because I thought it would get me attention."*

## Critics' Concerns

Alex's retraction reinforced concerns that critics have with his story and similar works of "heavenly tourism." Alex's dad said "we have the Scriptures as an infallible guide to evaluate everything we experience" and "anything that does not square with Scripture is counterfeit."[6] When the critics compare Scripture with the book, however, they find problems. The Bible says that God is Spirit (John 4:24), but the book says Alex saw God with a large, human-like body. In Jesus' story of the rich man and Lazarus, Abraham is reported as telling the tormented rich man in Hades that "between us and you a great chasm has been fixed, in order that those who would pass from here to you may not be able, and none may cross from there

---

4 Kevin and Alex Malarkey, *The Boy Who Came Back from Heaven: A Remarkable Account of Miracles, Angels, and Life Beyond This World* (Carol Stream, IL: Tyndale, 2010), 47. See similar statements on page 176.

5 Ibid., 213.

6 Ibid, 188–89. Similarly, *90 Minutes in Heaven* claims, "Don's testimony does not expand on or contradict any scriptural teachings on the afterlife" (p. 11).

to us" (Luke 16:26). The book, however, indicates that Alex saw a hole that goes from the outer room of heaven to hell.

Broadening out to the whole genre of afterlife travelogues, critics claim that in the Bible, visions of heaven, such as those experienced by the prophet Isaiah, the prophet Ezekiel, and the apostle John, are very rare and they are visions, not near-death experiences or purported journeys to heaven taken by dead people who return to tell about it. Hebrews 9:27 says, "It is appointed for man to die once, and after that comes judgment." So, critics say, we have no reason to believe that after dying and going to heaven people will come back to earth to describe it.[7]

Though Lazarus was dead for four days before Jesus resurrected him, much longer than the minutes or hours reported in recent books, we have no account from Lazarus about what he experienced during that time. The same is true in all the other biblical resurrections, such as the widow's son whom Elijah raised (1 Kings 17:17–24), the widow's son whom Jesus raised (Luke 7:11–17), or the many believers who came back to life after Jesus' death (Matt. 27:50–53). In none of those cases do we have a report of what these people experienced after they died, much less a detailed description comparable to the recent purported travelogues from heaven.

Critics also find fault with the overly familiar, almost nonchalant character of some of these reports of heaven that seem to lack reverence and awe. Jesse said he complimented Jesus on his sermon and put out a hand to comfort Jesus, who was welling up with tears of hurt. Colton said he was seated in a special little chair next to God

---

7  Heavenly travelogues go back to the medieval period, as documented by Jeffrey Burton Russell, *A History of Heaven: The Singing Silence* (Princeton, NJ: Princeton University Press, 1997), especially chapter 7. Perhaps most famously, around the year 1150, an Irish knight named Tondal reportedly toured heaven in a dream and his story influenced many in the Middle Ages. The genre of heavenly travelogues has multiplied at a rapid pace in the past twenty-five years, especially since Betty J. Eadie's bestseller *Embraced by the Light* (New York: Bantam, 1992). As long as they keep selling, such heavenly travelogues are likely to continue to proliferate in the years ahead.

the Holy Spirit. Alex said he chatted with several angels on a first-name basis and had many private conversations with God on his repeated trips to heaven. By contrast, when Isaiah saw God, he cried out, "Woe is me! For I am lost; for I am a man of unclean lips, and I dwell in the midst of a people of unclean lips; for my eyes have seen the King, the Lord of hosts!" (Isa. 6:5). After his vision of the glory of the Lord, Ezekiel said, "I fell on my face" (Ezek. 1:28), a reaction very similar to that of John, who reported that when he saw Jesus, the Son of Man, in heaven, "I fell at his feet as though dead" (Rev. 1:17).

Critics further point out that it is impossible to believe all these accounts of heaven because they contradict each other. Jesse said the Holy Spirit is not in heaven but on the earth, while Colton claimed that in heaven he sat next to the Holy Spirit, who was bluish in color. Don said people in heaven were the precise age they had been when Don last saw them on earth, with a wide variety of ages, including his elderly, white-haired grandfather. Colton, by contrast, reported that no one in heaven is old, with most people such as his great-grandfather appearing as younger versions of themselves. Colton said all the people in heaven look like angels, with lights over their heads and wings they use to fly, but Jesse, Don, and Alex reported no such winged or haloed humans.

John MacArthur speaks for many critics when he says, "It is seriously dangerous to listen to anyone who claims to know more about God, heaven, angels, or the afterlife than God himself has revealed to us in Scripture."[8] In the wake of Alex Malarkey's retraction and under pressure from some Southern Baptist leaders, LifeWay Christian Resources decided in the spring of 2015 to no longer sell books on heavenly visitations, though they're easily purchased from Amazon.

These books about supposed visits to heaven and back are intriguing and their widespread popularity (millions sold in dozens of languages) reflects the human longing to know more about heaven.

---

8  John MacArthur, *The Glory of Heaven: The Truth about Heaven, Angels, and Eternal Life*, 2nd ed. (Wheaton, IL: Crossway, 2013), 19.

Due to their tensions with Scripture and the way they contradict each other, however, such books cannot serve as reliable guides to what Christians believe about heaven. For that reason, this book has tried to avoid extra-biblical reports about what heaven is like and to focus instead on the hopeful message Scripture gives to us about what we *won't* find in heaven.

## A True Visit from Heaven and Back

While I have no direct experience of heaven and I'm skeptical of the fanciful and contradictory reports of those who claim to have been there, the Bible tells us about a person who did come from heaven to tell us about it. So, if we want to consult a trustworthy person with firsthand information about heaven, the Bible points us to what the Son of God had to say on the topic.

The Gospel of John tells us that before he became flesh and dwelt among us humans, the eternal Word of God was with God in the beginning, right at the Father's side (John 1:1–18). Jesus spoke of himself as the bread of God that came down from heaven (John 6:32–33, 41–42, 50–51). Just before his death, Jesus told his disciples that he was leaving the world and going to the Father (John 14:12, 28; 16:17, 28). Luke concludes his Gospel by telling how Jesus "left them and was taken up into heaven" (24:51). Then at the start of Acts we hear how "this same Jesus, who has been taken from you into heaven, will come back in the same way you have seen him go into heaven" (1:11). According to Paul (Eph. 1:20–21) and Peter (1 Peter 3:21–22) Jesus is now at the right hand of God in heaven, a place of great authority and power. Jesus will return someday from heaven with his mighty angels (1 Thess. 4:16; 2 Thess. 1:7). So Jesus dwelt in heaven before coming down to earth. After his earthly ministry, Jesus ascended back to heaven, and his followers have been promised Jesus will return from heaven. He's a bona fide expert on heaven!

It's impossible to summarize, in a short space, everything Jesus taught about heaven. So in the concluding paragraphs of this appendix we will simply sample a section from each of the four Gospels in order to get a sense for what the Son of God had to say about heaven.

Matthew 6 opens with Jesus advising his disciples: "Be careful not to practice your righteousness in front of others to be seen by them. If you do, you will have no reward from your Father in heaven" (6:1). People who make a public display of their giving and their praying are rewarded in this life by other people seeing them and honoring them. They're the ones gunning for pastor-of-the-year or philanthropist-of-the-year awards. By contrast, those who give and pray in private get their reward from the Father in heaven (6:1–8). Jesus says our prayers shouldn't be focused on gaining the admiration of a human audience, but instead should be directed to "our Father in heaven" (6:9), praying that "your will be done, on earth as it is in heaven" (6:10). We are to pray that in the same way that God's will is done in heaven (fully, without reservation or delay) that it be done here on earth too. So in these few verses from Matthew 6, Jesus teaches us that heaven is where God the Father dwells. The Father in heaven doesn't reward spiritual show-offs, but instead rewards those who are more secretive in their giving to the needy and in their praying to him. We should pray for God's will to be done on earth just as it is already done in heaven.

Mark 10 tells about Jesus' interaction with a man who claimed he kept God's commandments since he was a boy. Mark 10:21 says, "Jesus looked at him and loved him. 'One thing you lack,' he said. 'Go, sell everything you have and give to the poor, and you will have treasure in heaven. Then come, follow me.'" Jesus loved this man enough to put a finger on the one obstacle that kept him from following Jesus and having treasure in heaven. Later, when he explained the situation to his disciples, Jesus said, "No one who has left home or brothers or sisters or mother or father or children or fields for me and the gospel will fail to receive a hundred times as much in this present age: homes, brothers, sisters, mothers, children and fields—along with persecutions—and in the age to come eternal life. But many who are first will be last, and the last first" (10:29–31). In this small section of Mark 10, Jesus linked treasure in heaven with eternal life in the age to come, enjoyed by his followers. He also pointed to the shocking reversal when those who are first in this earthly age will be last in the heavenly age to come, and vice versa.

Luke 10 narrates how Jesus sent out seventy-two of his followers to heal the sick and preach about the kingdom of God. The seventy-two returned with joy, telling Jesus how "even the demons submit to us in your name" (10:17). While affirming their authority over powers of evil, Jesus warned his followers to "not rejoice that the spirits submit to you, but rejoice that your names are written in heaven" (10:20). As great as it is to see God's power at work through us, it is even greater to enjoy eternity in heaven. Then Jesus said, "I praise you, Father, Lord of heaven and earth, because you have hidden these things from the wise and learned, and revealed them to little children" (10:22). Jesus teaches that God the Father is the Lord of heaven and earth. God reigns over all of creation, and he chooses to reveal his ways to those who trust him with a simple, child-like faith.

John 3 records Jesus' encounter with a Pharisee named Nicodemus. Jesus told him that no one could see God's kingdom unless that person was born again or born from above (3:3, 7). When Nicodemus failed to understand, Jesus said plainly, "No one has ever gone into heaven except the one who came from heaven—the Son of Man" (3:13). When Jesus spoke about being born from above or about heavenly things, he was speaking about what he knew firsthand. A little later in the chapter the point is reinforced that "the one who comes from heaven is above all. He testifies to what he has seen and heard" (3:31–32). Since he had existed in heaven eternally, Jesus knew what he was talking about! But in his ministry on earth, Jesus explained, "The Son of Man must be lifted up, that everyone who believes may have eternal life in him" (3:14–15). As he said later, "I have come down from heaven not to do my will but to do the will of him who sent me" (6:38). And the Father's will was that Jesus would lay down his life for others, dying for their sins (10:11; 15:13). Jesus taught that he came down from heaven so that everyone who believes in him can have eternal life—a life full of joy and blessing with him, in God's presence forever. If we're looking for reliable testimony about heaven, the best person to look to is Jesus Christ. He has much to teach us about heaven in the Gospels of Matthew, Mark, Luke, and John.

## For Individual Reflection or Group Discussion

1. As you consider the first three stories summarized in this appendix (Jesse, Don, and Colton), do you find yourself trusting or skeptical of their reports of what heaven is like? Why?

2. What do you think are the strongest points made by the critics of people's supposed travel to heaven and back? Explain.

3. What stands out to you most from the final section on what Jesus had to say about heaven?

4. If you knew that this was the final year of your earthly life, would you make any changes in your life or do anything differently to prepare for the afterlife?

# Appendix 2

# A Dozen Common Questions about Heaven

WILL THERE BE ANIMALS IN HEAVEN, including my pets? In the age to come, people wonder, what age will we be, or will age even be a dimension of our existence? Will we wear clothes in heaven, and if so, will they have variety or be one-size-fits-all white robes? These are just a few of the questions about heaven that I cannot answer definitively. The fact is that many of our questions about the afterlife will not be answered with certainty until we experience it for ourselves.

On the one hand, in our musings about heaven we should be humble because "no human mind has conceived the things God has prepared for those who love him" (1 Cor. 2:9). As finite and fallen creatures, we have a limited and often erroneous understanding of the things of God. On the other hand, we need not despair but should fully affirm "the things God has revealed to us by his Spirit" (1 Cor. 2:10). God has graciously revealed what we really need to know about heaven.

For twenty-two years, I have had the privilege of serving as a professor of theology at Malone University. Here in my office I am surrounded by the wisdom of other Bible scholars and theologians, whose books I gratefully consult on a regular basis. With their help, in this final appendix I take a stab at twelve questions about heaven. Those who are not interested in the finer, technical points of theology may choose to read from these dozen questions selectively.

## Appendix 2. A Dozen Common Questions about Heaven

### 1. What does the Bible mean by "heaven"?

Most English Bibles use the word "heaven" to translate the Old Testament Hebrew word *shamayim*, which has a sense of "the heights" and the New Testament Greek word *ouranos*, which has a sense of "what is raised up." So heaven generally refers to "what is above." More specifically, heaven can mean what we usually call the sky, the immediate atmosphere that surrounds the earth, where birds fly and clouds produce rain (Deut. 11:16–17; Matt. 16:2–3). It can also mean what we usually call space, the celestial heavens, where the sun, moon, and stars are (Gen. 1:14–19; Acts 2:19–20). Lastly, there is the spiritual meaning of heaven, where God and holy angels dwell and to which we direct our prayers (1 Kings 8:30–49; Matt. 6:9–10).

The Bible provides its readers with clear directions concerning each of the three meanings of heaven. In the Old Testament God's people are commanded to obey him so he will continue to send rain from heaven ("the sky") for their crops (Deut. 28:1, 12, 15, 23). The people are also commanded not to consult the heavens ("stars in outer space"), but instead to look to the Lord who made the heavens (Isa. 44:24–26; 45:12–13; 47:13–15). In the New Testament, God's people are told to not just orient their lives around this world but to focus themselves on the unseen, eternal world "above" (2 Cor. 4:18; Col. 3:1–4). Heaven, we are told, is the final destiny of those who trust in the Lord and live by faith (Heb. 11:13–16; 1 Peter 1:3–5). In this book, the focus has been on the third meaning of heaven, the place where God dwells with his angels and his people.

### 2. What does it mean that "God dwells in heaven"?

In the Old Testament, we frequently read of God looking down from heaven. Moses is reported as asking the Lord to "look down from heaven, your holy dwelling place, and bless your people Israel" (Deut. 26:15). Similarly, Isaiah asks the Lord to "look down from heaven and see, from your lofty throne, holy and glorious" (63:15). Psalm 33:13–14 says "from heaven the Lord looks down and sees all mankind; from his dwelling place he watches all who live on earth." In the New Testament, Jesus warns that those who practice their righteousness publicly in order to be seen by other people will have no reward "from your Father in heaven" (Matt. 6:1), and Jesus teaches his disciples a model prayer addressed to "our Father in heaven" (Matt. 6:9).

So throughout the Bible heaven is depicted as the dwelling place of God. But the Bible also teaches that God existed before he created the heavens and the earth (Gen. 1:1; John 17:5). While God is often pictured as dwelling in heaven, the Bible teaches that "the heavens, even the highest heaven, cannot contain you" (1 Kings 8:27; 2 Chron. 6:18). So while there is a special sense in which heaven is God's throne (Isa. 66:1; Matt. 23:22), the full biblical teaching is that God is in no way limited to dwelling in heaven but is present everywhere (Ps. 139:7–12; Jer. 23:23–24).

### 3. What exactly are "the new heavens and the new earth"?

The only Old Testament mention of "new heavens and a new earth" is found at the end of the book of Isaiah, in 65:17 and again in 66:22. Here the Lord promises to create an enduring new heavens and a new earth in which the former things will not be remembered. The New Testament also has two references to a new heaven and a new earth. Revelation 21:1 reports John's vision of "a new heaven and a new earth, for the first heaven and the first earth had passed away." Second Peter 3:13 says that "in keeping with his promise we are looking forward to a new heaven and a new earth, where righteousness dwells."

The preceding verses in 2 Peter 3:10–12 say that "the heavens will disappear with a roar; the elements will be destroyed by fire, and the earth and everything done in it will be laid bare" and "that day will bring about the destruction of the heavens by fire, and the elements will melt in the heat." For this reason, some Christians believe that the current heavens and earth will be totally destroyed and then replaced by a totally new heavens and new earth, created from scratch. In this view, the current heavens and earth will literally pass away (Matt. 5:18; 24:35; Rev. 21:1).

Other Christians have concluded that the Greek word John and Peter use for new (*kainos*) refers to the current heavens and earth being radically renewed or "made new" in the sense of being radically transformed, rather than completely destroyed and replaced. This second view appears to be supported by (a) the continuity between Christ's earthly body and his resurrection body (Luke 24), which is the pattern for Christians' resurrection bodies in the afterlife (1 Cor. 15) and (b) the picture in Romans 8:21 of how "the creation itself will be liberated from its bondage to decay." On this view, the fire spoken of in 2 Peter 3 is a purifying, refining fire, with the language of "destruction" (or "dissolving") referring to a thorough cleansing, not an eradication.[1]

What we know for sure is that the new heavens and the new earth are a great thing that God has promised to his people (Rev. 21:1), a place where righteousness dwells, and something worth looking forward to (2 Peter 3:13). Since the biblical phrase "the heavens and the earth" refers to the whole universe (Gen. 1:1; Acts 14:15; 17:24), we know that in some way the whole universe will be made new. In the afterlife, the new heavens and the new earth will be, in Michael Horton's words, "one cosmic sanctuary of everlasting joy."[2] While technically "heaven" as the current dwelling place of God is not quite the same as the future "new heavens and new earth" promised to God's people, this book has followed common convention by often using the single word "heaven" to refer to the lengthier "new heavens and new earth" that await us in days ahead.

---

1  J. Richard Middleton, *A New Heaven and a New Earth* (Grand Rapids: Baker, 2014), esp. 189-200.

2  Michael Horton, *The Christian Faith* (Grand Rapids: Zondervan, 2011), 915.

## 4. What precisely is "the holy city, the new Jerusalem"?

As an encouragement to the readers, perhaps including some who were considering returning from Christianity to Judaism, the author of Hebrews writes: "You have come to Mount Zion, to the city of the living God, the heavenly Jerusalem" (12:22). The heavenly Jerusalem, or city of God, is associated with "thousands upon thousands of angels in joyful assembly" and with "the church of the firstborn, whose names are written in heaven" (12:22–23). The heavenly Jerusalem, then, is a gathering of joyful angels and people whose names are written in heaven. The emphasis here is not so much on a physical location as it is on those who "have come to God" and "to the spirits of the righteous made perfect" and "to Jesus the mediator of a new covenant" (12:23–24).

Revelation 21:2 records how John saw "the holy city, the new Jerusalem, coming down out of heaven from God, prepared as a bride beautifully dressed for her husband" (see also Rev. 21:10). Four characteristics of this city stand out. First, it is holy, or untainted by sin, which makes sense because God is holy and in their glorified state God's people will be perfectly holy. Second, it is a new Jerusalem, bringing to mind God's dwelling place through much of Israel's history and God's fulfilled promises to his people (Isa. 52:1–10). Third, the city comes down out of heaven from God (see also Rev. 3:12). God's remedy for the evil earthly city of Babylon is the holy heavenly city of Jerusalem. Fourth, the "city" is described in personal, human terms, "as a bride adorned for her husband," an apparent allusion to God's people (Isa. 62:5; Rev. 19:7–9; 21:9–10).

Revelation 21:3 highlights a key characteristic of the holy city, namely, that it is the dwelling place of God and his people. "Behold, the dwelling place of God is with man. He will dwell with them, and they will be his people, and God himself will be with them as their God." This city points us, with great hope, to "the fellowship of God with his people in an actual new creation."[3]

---

3   G. K. Beale, *The Book of Revelation: A Commentary on the Greek Text* (Grand Rapids: Eerdmans, 1999), 1045.

In describing the holy city that comes down out of heaven, the final chapters of the Bible bring together images from the Garden of Eden, the city of Jerusalem, and the cubical Holy of Holies within the tabernacle and temple. It is a holy, garden-like city, which communicates to readers that as it had been in the earthly garden in Eden, and in the earthly temple in Jerusalem, so it will be in the heavenly Jerusalem or holy city—God will rule over and dwell with his people!

**5. When God's people die, do they go straight to heaven, and is that the same as paradise?**

When Jesus was crucified, it was not a solo event. He was joined by two criminals (Luke 23:32–33). One of the criminals recognized that while he was guilty, Jesus was innocent (Luke 23:41). This believing criminal asked Jesus to remember him when he came into his kingdom, and Jesus famously replied, "Truly I tell you, today you will be with me in paradise" (Luke 23:42–43).

In the Old Testament the term "paradise" described a forest, orchard, garden, or park (Neh. 2:8; Eccl. 2:5; Song of Songs 4:13). The Greek translation of the Old Testament uses "paradise" to refer to the garden of Eden (Isa. 51:3; Ezek. 28:13), and by the time of the New Testament it was commonly used to refer to the place where God's people go in the afterlife, or heaven. That explains how the apostle Paul could equate being caught up to the "third heaven" (see question 1) with being caught up to paradise (2 Cor. 12:1–4). Likewise John could speak of overcomers having the right to eat from the tree of life in the paradise of God (Rev. 2:7), picturing the perfect fellowship between God and his people in the afterlife. This helps us make sense of Jesus' promise to the believing criminal that after his death "today you will be with me in paradise."

Paul also anticipated that upon his death he would "depart and be with Christ, which is better by far" (Phil. 1:23). Paul looked forward to the time when he would "be away from the body and at home with the Lord" (2 Cor. 5:8). Apparently the fullness of bodily resurrection awaits a future time, but believers can find comfort in Jesus' promise and in Paul's expectation that God's people will be with Jesus after they die, in his immediate presence in a blessed state. Closely related to what we noted at the end of question 3, paradise, or heaven, as the place where God's people go to be with him after they die, is not technically quite the same as the future "new heavens and new earth," which God's people will inhabit in our resurrected bodies.

## 6. Can we be so heavenly minded that we're no earthly good?

Some people claim that if we think too much about heaven, we will not pay attention to what we should do on earth. The communist revolutionary Karl Marx famously stated that religion "is the opium of the people." His comrade Vladimir Lenin echoed Marx's idea in asserting that "those who toil and live in want all their lives are taught by religion to be submissive and patient while here on earth, and to take comfort in the hope of a heavenly reward."

Does focusing on heaven keep us from doing what we should on earth? Christian theologian C. S. Lewis argued the opposite, that "if you read history you will find that the Christians who did most for the present world were just those who thought most of the next. . . . [They] all left their mark on earth, precisely because their minds were occupied with heaven."[4] Jerry Walls concurs that "many of those who have taken the hope of eternal life as their paramount concern have also worked diligently to reform society and bring a foretaste of heaven to life on earth."[5]

The apostle Paul famously told the Colossians to "set your minds

---

4   C. S. Lewis, *Mere Christianity* (New York: Macmillan, 157), 104.

5   Jerry L. Walls, *Heaven: The Logic of Eternal Joy* (New York: Oxford University Press, 2002), 200.

on things that are above, not things that are on earth" (3:2). Does this mean we'll be no earthly good? If we follow the rest of the chapter, we see that, to the contrary, "heavenly mindedness" (3:1–4) should be accompanied by ridding ourselves of vices (3:5–11), living virtuously (3:12–14), worshiping heartily (3:15–17), having orderly and loving households (3:18–21), and working vigorously and faithfully (3:22–25). So in the New Testament we see that Jesus' followers are encouraged to be so heavenly minded that they are of the greatest possible earthly good, actively pursuing and promoting what is right in this life. Far from being a distraction, heaven can motivate us to live well right now, giving us a laser-like focus on those earthly tasks that are of eternal importance.

### 7. How can God's people be sure that heaven is real?

There is a sense in which, during this life, God's people must "live by faith, not by sight" (2 Cor. 5:7). In this life, we do not yet see God in heaven directly since God is normally invisible to our visual senses (1 Tim. 1:17; 6:16). So, God's people do not typically know that heaven is real by sight, but must live in the realm of faith, trusting what God has told us. But it is interesting that in his very next breath, Paul says, "we are confident, I say, and would prefer to be away from the body and at home with the Lord" (2 Cor. 5:8). Paul is so confident of the good things that await him in heaven that he would *prefer* to be away from the body and at home with the Lord!

Paul also says that "meanwhile we groan, longing to be clothed instead with our heavenly dwelling" (2 Cor. 5:2). Here, Paul speaks of not just a groaning to be delivered from the troubles of our present existence, but a groaning for glory, when we will see Jesus Christ and be clothed with a heavenly body. In the midst of this groaning, Paul's certitude that heaven is real is so high that he speaks of "knowing it." In his words, "we know that if the earthly tent we live in is destroyed, we have a building from God, an eternal house in heaven, not built by human hands" (2 Cor. 5:1). Rather than dwelling in flimsy, flawed temporary tents, God's people will one day live in permanent houses from God—imperishable, immortal spiritual bodies (1 Cor. 15:49–53).

But has God given us any assurance that heaven is real? Paul answers that God "has given us the Spirit as a deposit, guaranteeing what is to come" (2 Cor. 5:5; see also Eph. 1:14). The Holy Spirit is sort of like earnest money or a first payment (a pledge, like an engagement ring) that indicates what God's intentions are for his people. If God has put down earnest money or made a pledge, God's people can take it to the bank. The Spirit in us now assures us that heaven is real.

### 8. Will God's people personally know our family, friends, loved ones, and others in heaven?

Many people look forward to being reunited in heaven with loved ones who have already passed on from this life. Others claim that this sort of yearning to be with family and friends in heaven is misplaced because heaven is all about God. My answer to this question is closely related to what I said earlier in chapter 6 about loving God and loving people, both on earth and in heaven.

The first and the greatest commandment is to love God with our whole selves. As noted in chapter 6, the biblical pictures of heaven show that God is at the center of it all. So it would be wrong to place so much emphasis on being with our loved ones that we forget about being with God. But those two things need not compete with each other, as though more of one meant less of the other. The joy of heaven includes fellowshiping with both God and God's people.

In the story of Genesis 2, even though the first man, Adam, was in a perfect environment and had a perfect relationship with God, it was not good for him to be alone (2:18). People were created as social beings who need each other, as we see with the creation of the first woman (2:20–25). Our social natures are reinforced by Jesus' teaching that the afterlife includes many taking our "places at the feast with Abraham, Isaac and Jacob in the kingdom of heaven" (Matt. 8:11). Jesus also tells us that "at the resurrection people will neither marry nor be given in marriage" (Matt. 22:30). So our relationships in heaven won't be an exact replica of what they were on earth. On the other hand, King David seems to be comforted and encouraged by the expectation that in the afterlife he would see his son, who died just a week after birth (2 Sam. 12:18–23). Putting all of this together, it appears that in heaven people will be recognizable as individuals (Abraham, Isaac, Jacob, David's son). And Christians can find comfort in knowing that in heaven they will see those who died before them (1 Thess. 4:13–18), but the Bible never describes exclusive nuclear family gatherings in heaven, probably because we are part of God's larger, extended family there (Luke 8:19–21; 1 Thess. 4:10).

### 9. What will people's resurrection bodies be like in the new heavens and the new earth?

Jesus' followers are told that he "will transform our lowly bodies so that they will be like his glorious body" (Phil. 3:21). John confirms that "when Christ appears, we shall be like him" (1 John 3:2). So our resurrection bodies will be like Jesus' resurrection body. Jesus' resurrection body still had flesh and bones and could be touched (Luke 23:39). He could be touched and seen (Luke 23:39–40; John 20:27). He talked with his disciples and ate a piece of broiled fish with them (Luke 23:42–43). Peter was an eyewitness "who ate and drank with him after he rose from the dead" (Acts. 10:41). Jesus remained recognizably himself (Luke 24:31, 35). So, presumably, in our resurrected state we will be recognizable and have the ability to talk, eat, drink, be touched and seen. There will be a measure of continuity between our bodies now and after the resurrection.

On the other hand, in his resurrected state Jesus also disappeared suddenly from people's sight (Luke 24:31) and suddenly appeared among his followers in a way that startled them (Luke 24:36–37). John recounts an incident in which, "when the disciples were together, with the doors locked for fear of the Jewish leaders, Jesus came and stood among them and said, 'Peace be with you!'" (John 20:19). Then John reports that "a week later his disciples were in the house again, and . . . though the doors were locked, Jesus came and stood among them and said, 'Peace be with you!'" (John 20:26). So when we are raised, "we will be changed" (1 Cor. 15:51–52) in such a way that there will also be a measure of discontinuity between our bodies now and after the resurrection.

As with most questions about heaven, we don't know everything we might like to know, but we do know that "the body that is sown is perishable, it is raised imperishable; it is sown in dishonor, it is raised in glory; it is sown in weakness, it is raised in power; it is sown a natural body, it is raised a spiritual body" (1 Cor. 15:42–44). For more details, we will just have to wait and see!

## 10. What practical impact can heaven have on my life now?

Hebrews 11 narrates how Abel, Enoch, Noah, Abraham, Isaac, Jacob, Sarah, and other believers in the Old Testament "did not receive the things promised; they only saw them and welcomed them from a distance, admitting that they were foreigners and strangers on earth" (11:13). What kept them going? "They were longing for a better country—a heavenly one" (11:16).

In his first letter, Peter addressed God's people as "exiles" (1:1) or those who are not fully at home in this life. He also urged Jesus' followers to "live out your time as foreigners here in reverent fear" (1:17) and "as foreigners and exiles, to abstain from sinful desires" (2:11). Rather than indulging ourselves now or building up temporary treasures, Peter focuses his readers on the "inheritance that can never perish, spoil or fade . . . kept in heaven for you" (1:4).

That is not to say that we should not enjoy life right now, since God showers us with many good things (James 1:17) and "richly provides us with everything for our enjoyment" (1 Tim. 6:17). But it is to say that we should not become so comfortable in this life that we fail to long for Christ's appearing and the world to come (2 Tim. 4:8). In the words of C. S. Lewis, "our Father refreshes us on the journey with some pleasant inns, but will not encourage us to mistake them for home."[6]

Those who are persecuted for Jesus' sake know they are not yet home, but in the meantime Jesus tells them to "rejoice and be glad, because great is your reward in heaven" (Matt. 5:12). Peter also says that because "the end of all things is near" Jesus' followers should pray, love each other deeply, and be "faithful stewards of God's grace in its various forms" (1 Peter 4:7–10). A heavenly perspective spurs us to be faithful with everything God has entrusted to us in this life, so that one day the Lord may say to us, "Well done, good and faithful servant!" (Matt. 25:21, 23).

## 11. Will everyone go to heaven?

John the Baptist describes Jesus as "the Lamb of God, who takes away the sin of the world" (John 1:29). If Jesus takes away the sin of the world, won't the whole world be saved? Paul also says, "God was reconciling the world to himself in Christ, not counting people's sins against them" (2 Cor. 5:19). If God has reconciled the world to himself and doesn't count people's sins against them, won't everyone go to heaven? Ten more passages people cite to support the view that all will go to heaven include John 12:32; Acts 3:21; Romans 5:18; 11:32; 1 Corinthians 15:22; Ephesians 1:9–10;

---

6  C. S. Lewis, *The Problem of Pain* (New York: Macmillan, 1962), 115.

Philippians 2:10–11; Colossians 1:19–20; 1 Timothy 4:10; and Hebrews 2:9.

But Jesus also said that when he returns, he "will separate the people one from another as a shepherd separates the sheep from the goats" (Matt. 25:32), with the final result that the goats go away "to eternal punishment" but the sheep "to eternal life" (Matt. 25:46). If some people go to eternal punishment, how can they also go to heaven? Paul says, "those who do not know God and do not obey the gospel of our Lord Jesus" will "be punished with everlasting destruction and shut out from the presence of the Lord and from the glory of his might" (2 Thess. 1:8–9). How can that possibly fit with the idea that these people will go to heaven? Ten more passages people cite to support the view that not everyone will go to heaven include Matthew 7:13–14; 8:12; 26:24; Mark 3:29; Luke 16:19–31; John 3:16–18; 5:28–29; Romans 2:5; 9:22; and Revelation 21:8.

In considering all these passages and accounting for the message of the whole Bible, it is evident that, hard as it is for us to hear, not everyone will go to heaven. While Jesus' death makes salvation available to anyone who would believe in him, it is when people trust in Jesus that they actually experience salvation. Christians have the great privilege of telling everyone the good news about Jesus, confident that anyone who comes to Jesus and believes in him will have eternal life (John 6:37–40).

## 12. How do people go to heaven?

People have a lot of different ideas about this question. Since everything, including heaven, was created by God's Son (Col. 1:16; Heb. 1:2), and since God's Son came down from heaven to give life to the world (John 6:50–51), it's important to consider what God's Son says about heaven.

Matthew records that right from the start of his public ministry, "Jesus began to preach, 'Repent, for the kingdom of heaven has come near'" (Matt. 4:17). No matter how good or bad a person is, Jesus says, "unless you repent, you too will all perish" (Luke 13:3, 5). Repentance requires radical change, turning away from sin and turning toward God's Son and his heavenly kingdom. When that happens, Jesus says, there is "rejoicing in heaven over one sinner who repents" (Luke 15:7).

In conjunction with repenting from our sins, Jesus proclaimed that we must also believe in him, a point stressed in the Gospel of John. Jesus says to Martha and to all of us today, "I am the resurrection and the life. The one who believes in me will live, even though they die" (11:25). People must respond to Jesus' challenging claim that "no one comes to the Father except through me" (14:6) and his warning that "if you do not believe that I am he [the one the Father sent from heaven], you will indeed die in your sins" (8:24). But John hopes for better things for those who read his Gospel, which he wrote for the express purpose that "you may believe that Jesus is the Messiah, the Son of God, and that by believing you may have life in his name" (20:31).

Repentance and belief go together. Jesus called people to "repent and believe the good news" (Mark 1:15). This was a pattern that Paul followed in his ministry to people from all religions, declaring "to both Jews and Greeks that they must turn to God in repentance and have faith in our Lord Jesus" (Acts 20:21). The Bible teaches that everyone who repents of their sins and trusts in Jesus as their Lord and Savior is a citizen of heaven (Phil. 3:21). Then we will enjoy perfect relationships with God and all of God's people in the perfect place Jesus has prepared for us (John 14:1–3).

## For Individual Reflection or Group Discussion

1. What are a few questions you personally have about heaven? Things you'd love to know?

2. Read Revelation 21–22. When you reflect on the descriptions of "the new heavens and the new earth" and "the holy city, the new Jerusalem," what especially jumps out to you? Explain.

3. In what sense do you honestly share or not share Paul's conviction that "to live is Christ and to die is gain" so "I desire to depart and be with Christ, which is better by far" (Phil. 1:21–23)?

4. In your own words, how would you answer the weighty questions at the end of the appendix about whether or not everyone will go to heaven and how people go to heaven?